KV-192-760

Norman Sullivan has been a driving instructor and driving school proprietor for over forty years, which makes him one of the most experienced driving instructors in the country. He is a Department of the Environment Approved Instructor, an RAC Registered Instructor, holder of a City and Guilds Further Teaching Certificate and a Member of the Institute of Advanced Motorists. He has also lectured on car mechanism and maintenance.

Car Maintenance complements Norman Sullivan's Fontana book about driving, *Road Test* (1978). Among his other books on driving are *The Learner Driver* (1963), *The Advanced Driver* (1963), *101 Driving Lessons* (1968) and *Are You a Skilful Driver?* (1975). He has also compiled a number of crossword puzzle books, and is the author of *Use Your Intelligence* (Fontana, 1978).

Norman Sullivan

Car Maintenance

Drawings by Illustra Design Ltd

Fontana Paperbacks

First published by Fontana Paperbacks 1979
Copyright © Norman Sullivan 1979

Set in Monotype Times

Printed in Great Britain by
Richard Clay (The Chaucer Press) Ltd, Bungay, Suffolk

To Dai and Barry

Contents

Acknowledgements

My thanks to the fifty drivers who allowed themselves to be pre-tested, and from whose results I have been able to evaluate an acceptable 'average' standard for comparison purposes. Thanks also to Eddie Lewis for his valuable assistance in the collection of these results. From this reasonably large sample the analyses and ratings at the end of this book have been made possible.

Finally, my thanks to Hull's Motors Ltd, of Stanford-le-Hope, Essex, for their co-operation and assistance.

Introduction

The ideal motorist is not simply a skilful driver who knows the Highway Code and is conversant with motoring laws and regulations, insurance requirements and so on; he or she also knows enough about the mechanics of the car to be able to carry out routine points of maintenance and repair, thus keeping the car in first-class condition, and to diagnose faults that must be put right by experts, in this way saving time and economizing on garage bills. The motorist who knows his car and how it works is likely to be a more confident driver, and therefore a better one: compared with the driver who is ignorant about cars he is less alarmed by the thought of an unexpected breakdown; his well maintained vehicle runs smoothly, allowing him to concentrate fully on the road; and the chances are that he derives more pleasure from driving.

I hope that the seven tests in this book will provide an enjoyable way of improving your knowledge of the car and its workings, and help you to become much more like that ideal motorist.

Each test is designed to check your knowledge of car maintenance, your ability to diagnose faults and to rectify them, and your knowledge of mechanical parts and functions. The explanations that follow each test are meant not only to justify the correct answers but also to act as instructional guides.

There are four types of question in the tests. Many of them have 'multiple choice' answers, of which only *one* is correct (the remaining, incorrect ones are known as 'distractors'). In another kind of question, you are asked to associate one list of items labelled with letters with another list labelled with numbers. In this case, *all* the lettered items must be associated with at least one of the numbered items; and in some of these questions, a lettered item can be associated with more than one of the numbered items. There are also 'true or false' questions in which four statements are made and each one should be marked either true or false. Finally, some questions require you to fill in a missing word or phrase.

Speed of answering affects your 'rating', for at the end you will have to add or deduct points on a time basis. (Remember, though, that it is better to give a correct answer after some thought than to give a wrong answer quickly.) Therefore, take a careful note of how long it takes you to complete each test. You can rest for as long as you wish between tests.

As soon as you finish each test, check your answers, and enter both the number of points you have scored *and* the time taken.

Do not be disappointed if, as you check your scores test by test, you appear to have low marks. Just persevere with *all* the tests, so that at the end you can calculate the *total* number of points scored throughout.

At the end of the book you will find the scores of fifty pre-tested drivers (and a simple formula from which you can assess your own 'rating'), and it is only when you have compared your score with theirs that you will know how well or badly you have done. *But do not refer to this until you have completed all the tests and read the explanatory notes.*

Finally to sum up:

1. Make sure you have pen or pencil ready and, if you do not wish to deface the book, a piece of paper.
2. Time yourself carefully on each test.

3. After each test check your answers and enter your score.
4. Read the explanations of each test before going on to the next one.
5. Do not be disappointed if you seem to have low scores. You will not know if they *are* low until you read the ratings analyses at the end.
6. If you do not know an answer, try to make an 'inspired guess', rather than leave it blank. (The odds against guessing correctly throughout any one of these tests are at least 10,434,456 to 1.)

Grays, Essex.   NORMAN SULLIVAN

Test 1

1 One object of the condenser is:

    (*a*) To prevent wet CB points from shorting ☐
    (*b*) To reduce arcing at the points ☐
    (*c*) To increase the voltage ☐
    (*d*) To provide an earth return ☐

2 Which of these could cause too rich a mixture:

    (*a*) Blocked air filter ☐
    (*b*) Partially blocked jet ☐
    (*c*) Leak in inlet manifold ☐
    (*d*) Faulty petrol pump ☐

3 Putting a car in gear and rocking it backwards and forwards with the ignition and handbrake off may cure:

    (*a*) Starter motor whirring ☐
    (*b*) Starter motor failing to turn ☐
    (*c*) Starter turning engine too slowly ☐
    (*d*) Jammed starter pinion ☐

4 Mark each of these statements as TRUE or FALSE:

    (*a*) On a four-cylindered engine the only objects of the flywheel are to smooth off the rotation of the crankshaft and to provide for part of the clutch mechanism.   TRUE/FALSE

   (*b*) A six-cylindered engine could have the firing-
       order: 1 4 2 6 3 5.   TRUE/FALSE

   (*c*) Adjustment of the handbrake is always made
       by adjusting the rear brakes.   TRUE/FALSE

   (*d*) The mixture control screw on a carburetter
       should be turned inwards to enrich the mixture.

                                             TRUE/FALSE

5 A fuse blows, and you do not have a replacement. As a
  temporary expedient, which of the following would you
  not use:

   (*a*) Silver foil from a cigarette packet wrapped
       round the old fuse   ☐

   (*b*) A piece of household fuse wire connected be-
       tween the two fuse terminals   ☐

   (*c*) A strand of wire unravelled from a piece of
       electrical flex   ☐

   (*d*) A thin nail to bridge the fuse terminals   ☐

6 You are driving along and notice that the temperature
  gauge registers 'hot' and the ignition warning light is on.
  Which of these would you suspect:

   (*a*) Broken fan belt   ☐
   (*b*) Faulty generator   ☐
   (*c*) Leaking radiator   ☐
   (*d*) Thermostat stuck closed   ☐

7 In a four-stroke engine an exhaust valve has just closed.
  Which stroke will the piston of that cylinder be on
  next:

   (*a*) Exhaust stroke   ☐
   (*b*) Compression stroke   ☐
   (*c*) Induction stroke   ☐
   (*d*) Power stroke   ☐

8 Could insufficient valve clearance cause:

(*a*) Too weak a mixture ☐

(*b*) Loss of compression ☐

(*c*) Too rich a mixture ☐

(*d*) Noisy tappets [ ]

9 Which statement or statements do you associate with (i) Valves, (ii) CB points, (iii) Plug points:

(*a*) Excessive clearance causes noise.

(*b*) Require periodical adjustment.

(*c*) Must be kept clear of oil.

(*d*) Insufficient clearance causes damage.

(i) _____

(ii) _____

(iii) _____

10 The object of bleeding the brakes is:

(*a*) To exclude air from the system ☐

(*b*) To exclude surplus fluid ☐

(*c*) To maintain the level of fluid ☐

(*d*) To ensure that the brakes pull off completely ☐

Check your answers from page 114 and enter here:

Total scored ☐ points

Time taken ☐ minutes

Now read the explanations of this test before continuing.

Explanations

1 Air is a very effective insulator against electricity, and to pass through even a very small air space the current must be pushed with considerable force ('voltage'). When the CB points are closed the low tension (LT) current supplied by the battery (usually 12 volts) passes through them and returns to earth. When they are open, small as the gap is between them, such little voltage is incapable of bridging the gap. But when the points *first begin to open*—in that split second from when they are fully closed to when there is the smallest possible gap between them—the current *tries* to jump across. This results in burning of the points through 'arcing'.

The condenser contains a number of layers of conducting material insulated from each other; it is therefore depicted on circuit diagrams like this:

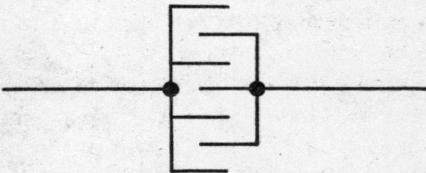

When the current finds its way barred by the air space developing between the points it realises that there is an easier journey—through metal (along which it is happy to travel) into the condenser. Here it becomes trapped!

It has no escape. Like a squirrel in a cage or a dog chasing its own tail, it dashes around, frantically looking for a way out. Finding none, it returns to the points. But although this merry little game takes only a small fraction of a second to play itself out, by the time it again reaches the points it finds it now has no possible line of escape there either, as the gap is too great for it even to attempt to leap across. Resigned to its fate, it returns to the condenser and finally makes its way back to earth, since the condenser is itself earthed.

The condenser acts as a *temporary* storage of electricity, and its main object is to prevent arcing (burning) at the points—or at any rate to reduce it (*b*). Another object of the condenser is to ensure an *instantaneous* collapse of the LT current when the points are open, and cause HT (high tension) current to be induced into the secondary winding.

(*a*) is an unsatisfactory answer, as wet CB points will short out anyway, with or without a condenser.

(*c*) Nor can it be claimed that it causes an *increase* of voltage—a distinction that belongs to the coil!

(*d*) True, the condenser *does* provide an earth return (once the current has finished roaming around inside it), but the earth return is provided for anyway by the fact that the fixed CB points is earthed, and it is illogical to claim that this is the object of the condenser.

2 A 'rich' mixture means that there is either too much petrol or too little air, and anything that could increase the former or diminish the latter could be responsible.

(*b*) A partially blocked jet would reduce the petrol content and cause a weak mixture.

(*c*) A leak in the inlet manifold would allow too much air to be mixed with the petrol and also weaken the mixture. (Incidentally, petrol might also escape through the leak, thus reducing the petrol content of the mixture.)

(*d*) The petrol pump is responsible for *delivering* petrol to the carburettor, and if faulty would hardly cause a *rich* mixture.

(*a*) A blocked air filter, on the other hand, would restrict the flow of air to the carburettor and so enrich the mixture.

3 A whirring starter motor may be due to dirt or rust on the starter pinion or quickthread. Often it will be found that perseverance with the starter will eventually get results, though excessive use of the starter should be avoided as this will drain the battery and overheat the starter motor.

The immediate remedy, especially if the car is causing an obstruction, may be to ask for help in pushing the vehicle; then it can be started in gear with the ignition on. This fault *must* be cured as soon as possible, as it will almost certainly recur—often at the most awkward moments. The starter motor must be removed and thoroughly cleaned. The pinion and thread may be lightly lubricated with machine oil or a light smear of graphite grease or powder.

(*b*) If the starter motor fails to turn when the starter is used it means that either current is not reaching it or there is insufficient current. The former could be due to loose battery connections or a loose connection at the starter motor; the latter would mean that the battery was not fully charged. It takes considerable output from the battery to start the engine, and although the battery might be strong enough to operate other electrical components it might not have sufficient charge to operate the starter.

(*c*) If the starter turns the engine, but not quickly enough to start it, this is also a sign that the battery is either not fully charged or that there is a loose connection.

(*d*) Here the starter pinion can be heard to be thrown into the starter ring, but fails to turn the flywheel, having jammed in position. This may be due to wear on the Bendix pinion or quickthread or wear on the teeth of the flywheel. As the flywheel will always tend to stop in more or less the same positions (when a piston is at the end of its compression stroke), certain teeth on the starter ring receive more wear than the others. If jamming is the result of worn teeth on the starter ring it is obviously likely to recur. The starter can often be freed again by putting the car into gear and rocking it backwards and forwards (making sure that the ignition and handbrake are both off). Usually when the pinion frees itself you will hear a welcome click as it jumps out of mesh with the starter ring. Should this fail it will be necessary to turn the squared end of the starter motor shaft with a suitable spanner, and if *that* fails, all that can be done is to remove the starter motor and rectify the fault.

4 (*a*) A flywheel has *three* functions, two of which are to form part of the clutch mechanism and to smooth off the rotation of the crankshaft. On a four-cylindered engine there would be a tendency for each piston to come to a momentary stop at the top and bottom of each stroke, just as if you were pedalling a bicycle without a chain; each time either foot reached the top or bottom there would be a tendency to stop pedalling for a moment. This would cause the engine to be very jerky. The flywheel stores the energy and carries the crankshaft smoothly over these 'flat' spots. With a six-cylindered engine this jerkiness would not prevail, since the piston strokes would 'overlap'; before any piston reached the top or bottom of its stroke another piston would be on its way up or down to give added thrust to the crankshaft.

But the third reason for a flywheel, even on a six-cylindered engine, is because the starter ring forms part of it. In other words, it is part of the *starting system*, and whether a four- or six-cylindered engine, this third object must be catered for.

(*b*) The normal firing order of a six-cylindered engine is: 1 5 3 6 2 4, just as the normal firing order of a four-cylindered engine is: 1 3 4 2. But there can be exceptions. An alternative firing order for four cylinders is: 1 2 4 3; the alternative firing order for six cylinders is: 1 4 2 6 3 5. It is easy to arrive at these alternatives, simply by taking the first number (1) from the front, placing it at the back, and then reading the whole sequence in reverse: 1 5 3 6 2 4 or 4 2 6 3 5 (with the 1 placed in front).

(*c*) Normally, adjustment of the rear brakes automatically adjusts the parking brake. If, in spite of adjusting the rear brakes (the linings of which are known to be in good condition), the handbrake has to be pulled on too far before becoming effective, the handbrake cable needs to be adjusted. This should be carried out according to the maker's handbook, which usually specifies how many notches the brake should be pulled up the ratchet in order to have the brakes fully on. There may be an adjusting nut with its face formed as a cam, or a wing nut at the base of the handbrake lever. Handbrake cables tend to stretch in time, when such an adjustment will be necessary, but most frequently the adjustment will be made at the rear brakes. Excessive force should not be used when applying the handbrake, as this will expedite the stretching of the cables.

(*d*) The mixture control screw (sometimes called the 'volume control screw' or the 'air adjustment screw') is turned outwards (anti-clockwise) to enrich the mixture. This allows more petrol to mix with the air supply.

5 Any of the first three answers are acceptable substitutes to get you out of immediate trouble, but you should obtain a proper fuse as soon as possible.

(*a*) If using *silver* foil, only one or two layers should be used. If a short occurs the silver foil will shrivel away.

(*b*) A piece of household fuse wire would be excellent, but make sure it is approximately of the same rating as the blown fuse.

(*c*) If you unravel a piece of flex, do not use more than one strand.

(*d*) On no account should you use a thin nail. This could be highly dangerous, as it will resist heat. The original fuse may have blown through a short, and as the short will still be there, the resistance of the nail could well cause a fire.

6 If the water is overheated *and* the ignition warning light is on, this means a fault in both the cooling system *and* the charging system.

(*b*) A faulty generator would certainly mean a breakdown in the charging system, causing the ignition warning light to come on, but the water temperature would not be affected.

(*c*) A leaking radiator would cause the water to overheat through loss, but could have no bearing on the charging system.

(*d*) Similarly, a thermostat stuck closed would cause overheating but would not influence the charging system.

(*a*) So we are left with the only thing that could affect both; that is, a broken fan belt. As the fan belt serves the dual purpose of driving the fan (to cool the water) and turning the generator, that alone must be responsible for the two faults at the same time.

7 One of the first things all students of car mechanism learn is the principle and operation of the 'Otto Cycle'— the four strokes of a piston and the operation of the valves during those strokes. This knowledge is put to

practical use in various checks and adjustments which are made to an engine, The Otto Cycle forms, as it were, the 'ABC' of car mechanics.

The first stroke is 'induction'. In this the inlet valve is open, allowing the mixture of petrol and air to be sucked in as the piston descends:

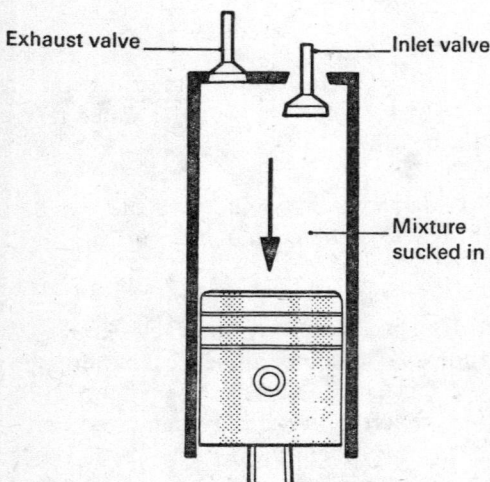

Exhaust valve _____   _____ Inlet valve

_____ Mixture sucked in

Both valves then close as the piston rises to compress the mixture. This is the 'compression' stroke:

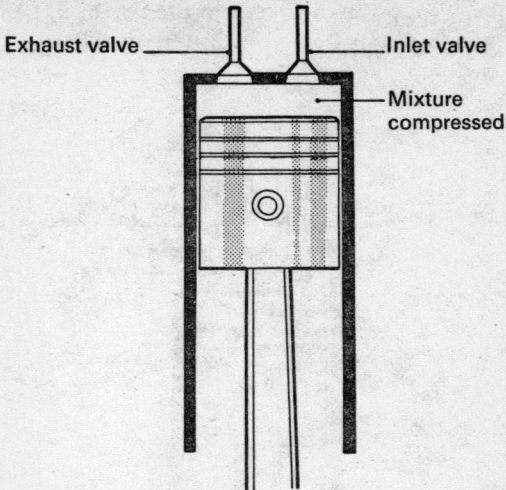

At this moment the spark occurs at the plug points, igniting the compressed mixture. The force of the explosion drives the piston down on its 'power' stroke:

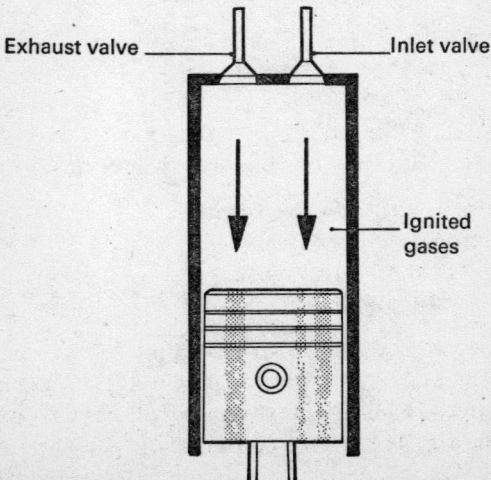

Assisted by the stored energy in the flywheel, the piston then rises under its own momentum, expelling the burnt gases through the exhaust valve, which is now open:

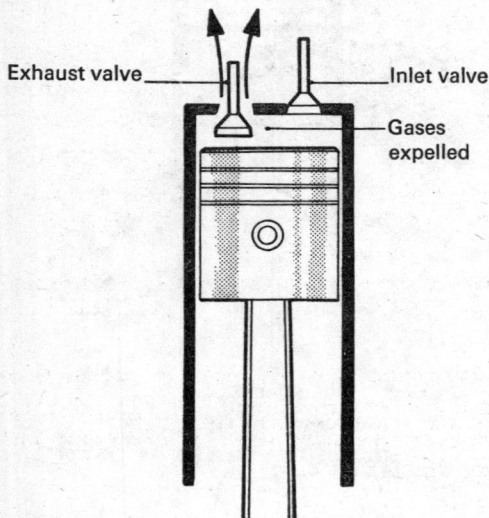

Exhaust valve

Inlet valve

Gases expelled

This cycle of operations is repeated indefinitely. Thus, the strokes, in the order in which they occur, are:

1 Induction (inlet valve open);
2 Compression (both valves closed);
3 Power (both valves closed);
4 Exhaust (exhaust valve open).

To answer the question, if an exhaust valve has just closed, then it follows that the piston has just completed its exhaust stroke. The next stroke will obviously be the induction stroke (*c*).

8 (*b*) Insufficient valve clearance could cause loss of compression for the following reason: when the valve becomes hot it will expand, and the correct clearance allows for this expansion (like the gaps between railway lines). If, however, the initial clearance is not enough, when the valve is fully expanded under heat it will be lifted slightly off its seating. On the compression stroke (see above), when *it is essential that both valves are fully closed*, full compression would not result.

(*a* & *c*) The strength of the mixture cannot possibly be affected, as it has already been determined by the carburettor before it reaches the inlet valve; the relative opening of the valve can only influence the *volume* of the mixture, not the *strength*.

(*d*) Noisy tappets is the result of *too much* clearance. When the valves are hot and fully expanded there is still unnecessary clearance, which will be heard in the form of light tapping.

9 (i) Excessive valve clearance would result in noisy tappets (see above) since, when the valves are hot and fully expanded, there would still be clearance between the rocker arms and the valve stems, causing a tapping noise.

This clearance should be checked at regular intervals, and certainly when noise develops.

Insufficient valve clearance can cause the valves to remain slightly open when they should be closed, resulting not only in loss of compression (and hence, power) but also in the valves becoming burned. Quite apart from being kept clear of oil, they must be kept well lubricated, and this is taken care of by oil mist rising from the sump when the oil is hot and, of course, by filling (in the case of overhead valves).

(ii) Noise cannot emanate from the CB (contact breaker) points gap being too great, nor can damage result if it is too small. The points must be checked regularly—about every 1,000 miles—because it is vital to smooth running to maintain the correct gap, which will vary as wear and burning of the points takes place, apart from the possibility of the retaining screw loosening.

Certainly, as with all electrical components, they must be kept clear of oil, since this would act as a conductor for the current, which must be broken at the instant the points open. For the same reason they must be kept clean, as dirt is also a conductor and will have the same adverse effect when the points open.

(iii) The plugs must be kept clean and free from oil; also they must be regularly checked, not only for these faults, but to make sure the correct gap is maintained. This gap will tend to widen, due to burning of the electrodes (making them thinner, and, hence, the gap wider) or narrow, due to carbon deposit forming on them—especially if running on the wrong mixture. Incorrect clearance between the points can cause neither noise nor damage, though it would affect the running of the engine.

10 (*a*) It is most important that air does not enter the hydraulic braking system. If it *does*—owing to the level of fluid in the reservoir having been allowed to fall too low, or if a pipeline becomes disconnected—it must be removed by 'bleeding'.

(*b*) As stated above, the object of bleeding is to exclude air—not 'surplus fluid'.

(*c*) As for 'maintaining the level of fluid', this is a routine point of maintenance which every driver should do by checking the level of fluid in the reservoir. Admittedly, if this level falls too low, bleeding will be necessary, but it could hardly be claimed that because of this the *object* of bleeding is to make up for a driver's negligence in maintenance. Also, of course, when bleeding, the level of fluid must be maintained in the reservoir throughout the operation.

(*d*) The pull-off springs account for the brakes pulling off completely after the hydraulic pressure is removed.

Test 2

1 Part of the inlet manifold passes close to, or touches, the exhaust manifold.

   This point is known as the _____

2 On *most* cars, approximately how much free play should there be in the clutch pedal:

   (*a*) None at all ☐
   (*b*) Up to one inch ☐
   (*c*) Half-way down ☐
   (*d*) Three inches ☐

3 An engine has the firing order: 1 3 4 2. Both valves of No. 1 cylinder are closed when:

   (*a*) No. 4 is on its induction stroke ☐
   (*b*) No. 2 is on its compression stroke ☐
   (*c*) No. 3 is on its power stroke ☐
   (*d*) No. 4 is on its compression stroke ☐

4 A gudgeon pin is found in:

   (*a*) A valve ☐
   (*b*) A timing pinion ☐
   (*c*) A piston ☐
   (*d*) A pulley ☐

5 The battery should be checked and, if necessary, topped up:

    (*a*) Every day ☐
    (*b*) Every week ☐
    (*c*) Depending on how much the car is used ☐
    (*d*) Every 1,000 miles ☐

6 Although the choke knob is pressed right in. the choke remains partly closed. This could cause:

    (*a*) White deposit on plug points ☐
    (*b*) Blue smoke from the exhaust ☐
    (*c*) Excessive petrol consumption ☐
    (*d*) Difficult starting when cold ☐

7 As a result of the fault in the ignition circuit shown below, would the engine necessarily:

    (*a*) Fail to start ☐
    (*b*) Misfire regularly ☐
    (*c*) Stop running ☐
    (*d*) Misfire irregularly ☐

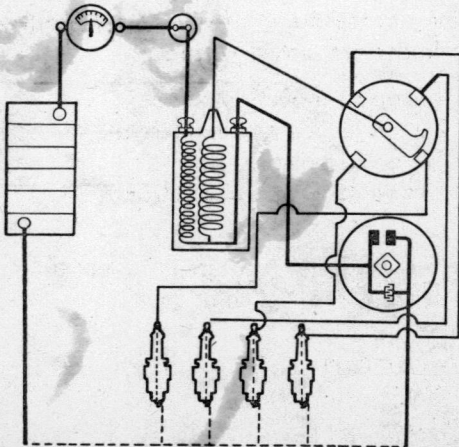

8 An SU electrical petrol pump makes a rapid ticking sound, but fails to deliver petrol.
The most likely reason is:

(*a*) No petrol in the tank ☐
(*b*) Bad earth connection to pump ☐
(*c*) Dirty contact points in pump ☐
(*d*) Loose electrical connection at pump ☐

9 Which of the listed symptoms do you associate with (i) Worn piston rings, (ii) Worn bearings, (iii) Leak in inlet manifold, (iv) Rich mixture:

(*a*) Pinking
(*b*) Spitting in carburettor
(*c*) Tapping
(*d*) Blue smoke from exhaust
(*e*) Knocking
(*f*) Black smoke from exhaust

(i) _____

(ii) _____

(iii) _____

(iv) _____

10 Fluctuating pressure registered on an oil gauge, especially when cornering, could mean:

(*a*) Broken oil pump
(*b*) Faulty pressure relief valve
(*c*) Worn bearings
(*d*) Insufficient oil in sump

Check your answers from page 114 and enter here:

Total scored ☐ points

Time taken ☐ minutes

Now read the explanations of this test before continuing.

Explanations

1 Part of the inlet manifold is very close to the exhaust manifold so that heat from the latter is conducted into the former to minimize condensation of petrol on the walls of the inlet manifold. This point, at which the two manifolds are closest to each other, is known as the 'hotspot'.

2 On most cars a clearance must be maintained in the clutch linkage between the adjustment nut and the operating fork, and this is reflected in free play in the clutch pedal. The clearance in the linkage varies from car to car and may be as little as .1 in. or as much as .25 in., resulting in about one inch of play in the pedal.

(a) No free play in the pedal (in other words, no clearance in the linkage) could soon lead to a slipping clutch which, if not attended to, could mean a new clutch—at no small cost. On some new cars the clutch release bearing is in constant contact with the diaphragm spring fingers and there is no clearance between the two. Thus there is no free play in the pedal, and adjustment is made when the clutch pedal is out of alignment with the brake pedal. However, the question specifies "most" cars, and certainly at the present time it is usual to maintain a clearance, as explained above.

3 'Firing order 1 3 4 2' means that the *power* strokes occur in that order. A matrix prepared on that hypothesis looks like this:

Cylinder	1	2	3	4
1st stroke	P			
2nd stroke			P	
3rd stroke				P
4th stroke		P		

The explanation of the Otto Cycle (see question 7 in Test 1) has shown that the strokes occur in this order:

1 Power
2 Exhaust
3 Induction
4 Compression

The remaining strokes are therefore these:

Cylinder	1	2	3	4
1st stroke	P	E	C	I
2nd stroke	E	I	P	C
3rd stroke	I	C	E	P
4th stroke	C	P	I	E

Both valves of No. 1 cylinder are closed when the piston is on *either* the compression stroke or the power stroke.

(*a*) When No. 4 is on its induction stroke, No. 1 is on its power stroke. This *could* satisfy the question and, as will be seen, it is the *only* answer that *does* satisfy the question.

(*b*) When No. 2 is on its compression stroke, No. 1 is on its induction stroke, when the inlet valve will be open.

(*c*) When No. 3 is on its power stroke, No. 1 is on its exhaust stroke, when the exhaust valve will be open.

(*d*) When No. 4 is on its compression stroke, No. 1 is again on its exhaust stroke, with the exhaust valve open.

4   A gudgeon pin forms an anchorage for the small end of the connecting rod and is contained inside the piston, as shown below:

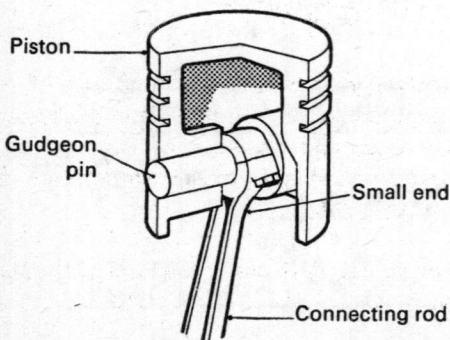

The small end of the connecting rod fits round the gudgeon pin, which is free to rotate in its seatings in the piston walls. This enables the connecting rod to swing like a pendulum as the piston moves up and down. If the gudgeon pin is fixed to either the connecting rod or the piston it is 'semi-floating'; if it is not fixed to either it is called: 'fully-floating'. The big end of the connecting rod is fixed to a crank pin on the crankshaft, so that the reciprocating motion of the piston is converted into rotary motion:

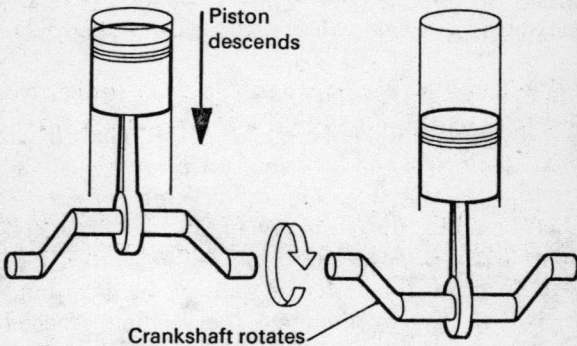

Piston descends

Crankshaft rotates

5 The electrolyte in the battery is made up of sulphuric acid and distilled water. Although acid does not evaporate, water does, and the rate of evaporation of the distilled water will vary as to the temperature and state of charge of the battery.

(a) It is not necessary to check the level of the electrolyte every day.

(b) But it should be done at weekly intervals. Topping-up is done with distilled water only, and the level should be maintained *just above* the top of the plates, which are visible when the filler caps are removed.

(*c*) It would be wrong to ignore this point of maintenance if the car is not in use. The distilled water will evaporate even under these conditions.

(*d*) Checking of the battery is best done on a time basis rather than on a mileage basis. Some drivers might cover 1,000 miles in a week, and this would conform to the standard laid down in (b). Other drivers might take as long as two months to cover 1,000 miles, and this would be far too long before carrying out this maintenance task.

6 First, consider what the choke is for. The carburettor mixes the petrol and air in correct proportions, and this mixture passes to the combustion chambers by way of the inlet manifold. But petrol evaporates very quickly, and in its passage along the inlet manifold small globules would tend to adhere to the walls of the manifold, with the result that by the time the mixture reached the combustion chambers it would have lost much of its petrol content. In other words, the final mixture would be too weak. In reducing this condensation and increasing vaporization of the petrol, heat plays a prominent part, and therefore the 'hotspot' is used to encourage induction of heat to the inlet manifold (see question 1). When the engine is stone cold, however, this will not help, and so the choke is introduced.

When the choke knob is pulled out it closes a butterfly valve in the carburettor air intake, thus excluding much of the air from the mixture. Even when this valve is fully closed, however, a very small quantity of air is still allowed through, otherwise there would be no 'mixture'—only liquid petrol. This ensures that, despite condensation of the petrol on its way to the engine, when it reaches the end of its journey there is still enough petrol content in the mixture to provide a satisfactory result. In other words, the choke has the effect of 'enriching' the mixture.

The engine quickly warms up and its own heat then contributes to vaporization; further use of the choke is now not only unnecessary but uneconomical and damaging to the engine, because of the excessive consumption of petrol (*c*) and the carbonic deposit which would be left on the points of the plugs.

(*a*) This deposit would be black in colour, whereas a white deposit would be a sign of the opposite extreme— too *weak* a mixture.

(*b*) When petrol is burned, *black* smoke results, and any smoke emerging from the exhaust as a result of the mixture being too rich would be black, and not blue.

(*c*) As explained, failure to press the choke knob completely home once the engine is warmed up will result in excessive petrol consumption. But the same effect is produced if, although the choke *knob* is pressed right in, the choke itself (the butterfly valve in the carburettor) remains even slightly closed, thus preventing the full quantity of air from mixing with the petrol. This is why a wise motorist will periodically check that the choke is fully open when the knob is pressed in.

(*d*) Since the object of the choke is to assist cold starting, it would hardly make it more difficult. It may well be that either because the weather is warm or the carburettor tuning does not require the use of the choke except in very severe weather conditions the *full* use of it would create difficult starting, even when the engine is not warmed up, but the question specifies that the choke remains *slightly* closed, and this would hardly affect the starting of the engine.

7 Careful examination of the circuit shows that there is a broken (or disconnected) plug lead.

(*b*) The effect of this would be that the engine would give a *regular* misfire.

(*c*) It would probably not stop running, as the three remaining cylinders would be able to keep it going,

(*a*) And it would not *necessarily* fail to start, though it would probably not start very easily, especially if cold.

(*d*) As the *same* plug would fail to fire each time the misfire would be regular, whereas if plug leads in general were loose or in bad condition the misfire would be irregular.

8 (*a*) As the contact points in an electrical petrol pump open and close they operate the diaphragm of the pump, and this pumps petrol to the carburettor as well as drawing it from the petrol tank. In normal use these points operate at regular, but somewhat infrequent, intervals. But if there were no petrol in the tank there would be no resistance against their movement, and they would operate very quickly and emit a loud 'hollow' clicking sound—usually regarded as a fairly sure sign that there is no petrol. An air leak in the pipe lines or unions, or faulty valves in the pump, would have the same result.

(*b*) A bad earth connection to the pump would either make the pump inoperative altogether or cause it to fail intermittently, according to whether the connection was broken or merely loose.

(*c*) The 'rapid ticking sound' referred to is made by the points operating very fast. Dirty contact points might cause them not to operate, but would not make them operate *fast*.

(*d*) A loose electrical connection at the pump would have a similar effect to a loose earth connection (*b*). Either the pump would fail or it would operate intermittently.

9 (i) The object of the piston rings is to make an air-tight seal between the piston and the cylinder. To obtain maximum compression (and hence power) this seal is as essential as the rubber plunger in a bicycle pump. The rings also provide an oil seal, preventing oil from escaping past the piston and into the combustion chamber. If they became worn, losing their springiness (which ensures this air-tight fit), apart from causing loss of compression, oil will get into the combustion chamber and become burned along with the petrol/air mixture. When oil is burned *blue* smoke results, and blue smoke from the exhaust is a sure sign that this is happening.

(ii) Worn bearings, however, will not allow oil to get into the combustion chambers, and so the colour of the smoke will not be affected. What *would* happen is that oil would leak through the bearings, causing a fall in pressure and a noise as vibration occurs. The resultant knock is due partly to the excessive clearance between the metal surfaces and partly to the breakdown of an oil cushion between the two. 'Knocking' is the only valid answer.

(iii) The mixture of petrol and air is carefully allowed for by the intricate design of the carburettor which, like a miniature computer, estimates the correct proportions of one to the other, mixes them together (in the mixing chamber) and then meters them out as required, according to the varying speeds. Unless the ratio of air and petrol is correct, the running of the engine will be affected. If there is too much petrol (or not enough air) the mixture will be too rich; if not enough petrol (or too much air) it will be too weak.

The carburettor is fixed on to the inlet manifold, and if there is a leak in the manifold too much air will be introduced into the mixture, so that by the time it reaches the jets it will be too weak. This might be evidence by 'spitting in the carburettor'—the effect of too weak a mixture.

(iv) A rich mixture (too much petrol) results in excessive petrol being consumed through burning in the combustion chambers, and this will be shown by black smoke from the exhaust. None of the other symptoms offered is valid

10 (*a*) A broken oil pump will fail to deliver oil under pressure and would register as either 'low' oil pressure or none at all.

(*b*) A faulty pressure relief valve would fail to let the oil by-pass the pump when maximum pressure is reached, so it would hardly register a *low* pressure.

(*c*) Worn bearings would register a low pressure, as oil would escape through them.

(*d*) If there is insufficient oil in the sump there will be a fluctuating reading on the oil gauge, especially when cornering, as the oil is swirled around inside the sump, causing it alternately to reach and then leave the oil pump inlet.

Test 3

1 You are inspecting a thirteen-year-old car with a view to purchase. Which of these would you consider to be the most important:

(*a*) Condition of the bodywork ☐
(*b*) Condition of the tyres ☐
(*c*) Condition of the engine ☐
(*d*) Condition of the upholstery ☐

2 You should check the oil level in the sump:

(*a*) With the engine cold ☐
(*b*) With the engine hot, immediately after switching off ☐
(*c*) With the engine running ☐
(*d*) With the engine warm, shortly after switching off ☐

3 On many cars the exhaust valve clearance should be greater than the inlet valve. This is because:

(*a*) The exhaust valve gets hotter ☐
(*b*) The inlet valve gets hotter ☐
(*c*) The exhaust valves must open more than the inlet valves ☐
(*d*) The exhaust valves need not open so much as the inlet valves ☐

4 'Thermo-syphon' refers to:

    (*a*) Cooling of water by the fan ☐

    (*b*) Air circulation through fins ☐

    (*c*) Circulation of water by pump ☐

    (*d*) Water circulation by convection ☐

5 If a battery lead became loose while driving at 40 mph the engine would:

    (*a*) Stop running ☐

    (*b*) Misfire irregularly ☐

    (*c*) Misfire regularly ☐

    (*d*) Continue to run normally ☐

6 Complete this sentence:

    'Too rich a mixture causes _____'

    (*a*) Pinking ☐

    (*b*) Spitting in the carburettor ☐

    (*c*) Uneven running when hot ☐

    (*d*) White deposit on plug points ☐

7 The plug leads have been removed from the distributor, but you have made a note that No. 1 takes this position:

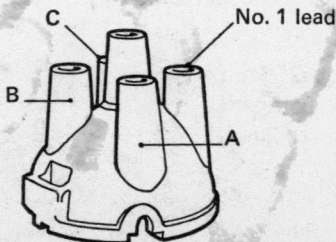

The rotor arm rotates anti-clockwise. How would you connect the remaining leads on a Ford 'Escort'?

A _____

B _____

C _____

8 Complete this sentence:
'The twisting force exerted on a shaft is known as
_____'

(a) Centrifugal force ☐
(b) Tension ☐
(c) Torque ☐
(d) Corkscrew action ☐

9 Where would you find a scraper ring:

(a) In a gearbox ☐
(b) On a piston ☐
(c) On a timing pinion ☐
(d) On a windscreen wiper blade ☐

10 The recommended gap at the sparking-plug points may vary according to the make of car. Is it *normally:*

(a) About .010 inch ☐
(b) About .025 inch ☐
(c) About .050 inch ☐
(d) About .005 inch ☐

Check your answers from page 114 and enter here:

Total scored ☐ points

Time taken ☐ minutes

Now read the explanations of this test before continuing.

Explanations

1 A man bought an old car on the strength of the fact that it had a recently fitted reconditioned engine. It ran beautifully, and he was delighted with it. Unfortunately, after a short time he discovered that the bodywork was eaten away in so many places that it was more like lacework. Apparently the previous owner had had an interesting time filling in the holes with plastic fillings, which eventually fell away, exposing the terrible state of the body. One year after he bought it he had to dispose of it—on the scrap heap. The bodywork was so far gone that the cost of making it good—even if this were possible—would have been far more than the car was worth. The consensus of opinion among many car dealers I have approached is that the bodywork is the most important consideration when buying an old car.

(*a*) Bodywork is all-important when buying an old car.

(*c*) A poor engine can often be improved, and may give the enthusiastic mechanic much pleasure in the process. In extreme cases a replacement engine, or short-engine, can be fitted.

(*b*) Tyres would be of minor importance, if they were the only drawback to buying it.

(*d*) The upholstery could be a more serious matter, depending upon how bad it was. Even so, upholstery can be renewed by firms specializing in this work.

2 The oil level in the sump should be checked every day if the vehicle is in constant use, even if the oil consumption of the vehicle is very low. A leak may develop at any time, and to run an engine without oil would be a very costly way of realising the necessity of this regular point of maintenance.

(*a*) When the oil gets hot—as it does when the engine is running—it also becomes thinner, and to check the oil level when the engine is cold (and the oil thicker) would not give a true indication of the quantity of oil circulating round a hot engine.

(*b*) Therefore, to ascertain the level under actual running conditions the oil level should be checked when the engine (and hence the oil) is warm. But to do so *immediately* after switching off would not offer a true reading, since much of the oil would still be clinging to various parts of the engine. A short time should be allowed for the oil to drop back into the sump.

(*c*) For the same reason it would be wrong to check the oil level when the engine is running. You want to check the amount of oil in the *sump*, not the amount which at that moment would be passing through the engine.

(*d*) The correct procedure is to make sure the car is on level ground, switch off the engine, wait for a short while to give the oil time to fall back into the sump, and then to check the level on the dipstick. Always remove the dipstick, wipe it clean, replace it, and then remove it again before taking a reading. The level shown on first removal will not be true, since oil will have splashed up the dipstick.

It must be admitted that most motorists check the oil

level first thing, before starting the engine. Although this is not strictly correct, it is infinitely better than neglecting to do so altogether.

3 In the Otto Cycle (see question 7 in Test 1), when a piston is on its induction stroke the inlet valve is open. This allows the mixture of petrol and air to enter the combustion chamber through the inlet manifold. This mixture is relatively cool (notice how cold your finger feels if you dip it into petrol). Therefore, the inlet valve *in itself* does not become very hot. But heat is induced into it because of its location in the combustion chamber and its proximity to the heat from the ignited gases.

It is a different story with the exhaust valve, through which the intensely hot burnt gases escape to the exhaust manifold. If one considers the tremendous heat generated from the combustion of the mixture within the confined space of the combustion chamber and the fact that this combustion may be taking place thousands of times every minute, it is easy to understand that the combustion chambers *and surroundings* become extremely hot. The exhaust valve usually gets hotter than the inlet valve although, in view of their close proximity, there is only a marginal difference between them. Since metal expands under heat, a clearance has to be maintained between the cam and tappet (or rocker arm and valve), otherwise, when hot, the valve would be lifted off its seating and not fully close.

(*a*) is the correct answer, because of the allowance which must be made for the greater expansion of the exhaust valve.

4 Hot water, like hot air, rises, and this characteristic is responsible for the circulation of the water through the

engine. The intense heat produced primarily in the combustion chambers and partially in the cylinders is conducted into the water which surrounds these parts of the engine. This water is housed in water pockets—or 'jackets'—which are bored into the cylinder block. As the water draws heat from the engine and itself becomes hot it begins to rise and makes its way into the header tank of the radiator through the rubber hose.

The object of the radiator core is to break up the water into small globules so that it descends slowly through the radiator, air being drawn through it by the fan. By the time the water reaches the lower tank it has been cooled by the air passing through the radiator, and hence can make its way through the engine again, starting cool (at the bottom) and finishing hot (at the top).

This movement (or 'circulation') continues all the time the engine is running, once the engine has warmed up. The diagram below makes this more clear.

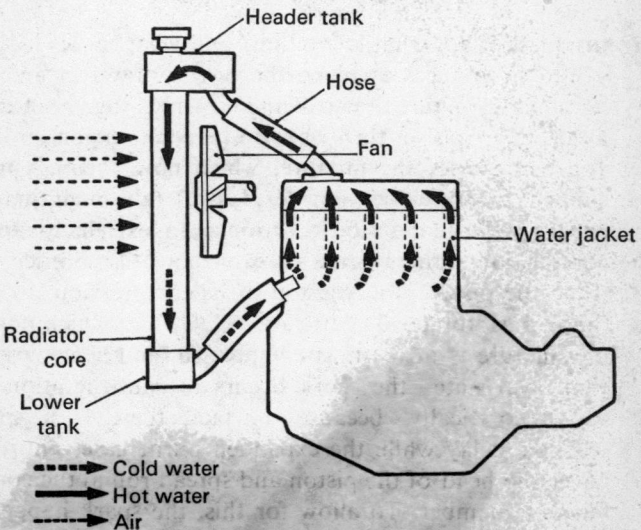

(*d*) 'Convection' means 'movement by heat', and so this is the correct answer.

5 Although a loose battery lead would cause difficult, or even impossible starting, when the engine is running fast (as it *would* be at 40 mph) the electrical current is taken care of by the dynamo or alternator. Therefore, if a battery lead became loose *while driving at this speed* the car would continue to run normally.

(*d*) This is the correct answer, since the question implies that the engine is not idling. When stopped, the engine might cut out since the battery would then be responsible for supplying the current to the coil.

6 (*a*) First of all, what is 'pinking' and what causes it?

On the induction stroke the piston draws in an in-flammable mixture of petrol and air which together form a 'gas'. The piston then rises on its compression stroke and compresses the mixture, which now becomes not simply 'inflammable' but 'explosive' (although many people prefer to describe its action as an 'extremely rapid combustion' rather than as an 'explosion'). Theoretically, when the piston is at the top of its compression stroke (known as 'top dead centre', or 'TDC')—at which point the mixture is in its most compressed (and hence, most explosive) state—the spark occurs to cause ignition. I say 'theoretically' because, in fact, there is a split second's delay while the expanded burnt gases entirely cover the head of the piston and spread round the combustion chamber. To allow for this, the spark happens fractionally *before* the piston reaches TDC, so that by the time it is in the TDC position the full force of the explosion can push the piston down on its power stroke, and hence *maximum* power is achieved.

If, however, the spark occurred prematurely, the force of the explosion would tend to push the piston down before it had actually reached the top; the stored energy of the piston would complete the upward stroke *against* the force of the explosion, and some of the force would thus be wasted. Moreover, the result would be a knock on the top of the piston, and this would be heard as a high-pitched metallic knock, known commonly as 'pinking', but more correctly as 'detonation'.

Although the grade of petrol would have an influence, the richness (or weakness) of the mixture could not lead to this. Perhaps in the very long term a *consistently* rich mixture would lead to a carbon deposit in the combustion chambers and on the piston heads, which would have the effect of reducing the size of the combustion chambers, causing premature detonation.

(*c*) But long before this, steps would have been taken to alter the mixture, since a rich mixture will cause uneven running, especially when hot.

(*b*) Spitting in the carburettor is a result of running on a *weak* mixture, and all drivers have experienced this at some time or other when starting off with a cold engine and the choke pushed in before the engine is sufficiently warmed up.

(*d*) The same fault—a weak mixture—will produce a white deposit on the plug points. A rich mixture, on the other hand, will leave a black (carbon) deposit on them.

7 The Ford 'Escort' has the firing order: 1 2 4 3, whereas most four-cylindered cars have the order: 1 3 4 2. Therefore, since the rotor arm rotates anti-clockwise, the remaining leads would be connected as indicated.

8 (*a*) Centrifugal force is the force by which a body revolving round a centre tends to fly outwards from the centre. When driving round a sharp bend it is important to ensure that the speed is not high enough for the car to come under the influence of this force, which would make it impossible to change direction, that is, steer round the bend.

(*b*) Tension is the pulling force exerted on a bar, etc.

(*c*) Torque—the twisting force exerted on a rotating shaft—is a very important consideration in mechanics. If one end of a shaft were made to rotate and the other end held firmly, there would be a tendency for the shaft to twist. If the force were great enough, the tendency would become a reality, and even a steel shaft could literally twist. If, for example, the rotation of a half-shaft at the road wheel were suddenly arrested by the other end of the shaft being held, this twisting could take place, and I have known of a half-shaft being broken in this manner by a learner driver inadvertently changing from top to bottom gear when intending to change from fourth to third: on release of the clutch pedal, the violent slowing down from about 25 mph to almost zero twisted the half-shaft so much that it sheared off in the differential, and examination of the splines showed that they were twisted almost into a spiral.

(*d*) 'Corkscrew action' simply means 'taking a spiral motion'.

9 The object of the scraper ring, which is fitted round a piston, is to prevent carbon and burning oil from reaching the other rings (the compression rings) and thus to prevent them from sticking with carbon; it also prevents the sparking plugs from sooting up. See diagram below:

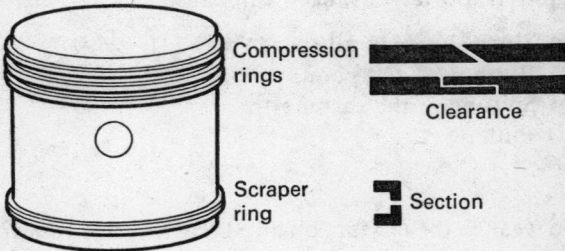

10 The recommended gap between the points of the sparking plugs is set out in the makers' handbooks, and varies from one car to another. But the variation will normally be between .020 in. and .030 in., and therefore (*b*) is the answer required.

   The gap should be checked about every 5,000 miles, and the plugs changed every 10,000 miles. When setting the gap do not attempt to move the central electrode, and when replacing do not overtighten. Make sure the metal gasket is in place and not broken.

Test 4

1 Ignition too far advanced can cause:

   (*a*) Sluggishness at all speeds   ☐
   (*b*) Burning of CB points   ☐
   (*c*) Spitting in the carburettor   ☐
   (*d*) Pinking   ☐

2 To weaken the mixture on an SU carburettor you would:

   (*a*) Move the jet needle upwards   ☐
   (*b*) Turn the jet nut downwards   ☐
   (*c*) Move the jet needle downwards   ☐
   (*d*) Turn the jet nut upwards   ☐

3 Approximately how much free play should there be in the fan belt:

   (*a*) None at all   ☐
   (*b*) About one inch   ☐
   (*c*) About two inches   ☐
   (*d*) About three inches   ☐

4 Which item or items do you associate with (i) Noisy engagement of bottom gear, (ii) Vibration in steering *at certain speeds*, (iii) Increased engine speed not giving a corresponding increase in road speed, (iv) Whine when clutch pedal is used:

(*a*) Engine running too fast
(*b*) No free play in clutch
(*c*) Front wheels out of balance
(*d*) Too much play in clutch
(*e*) Faulty spigot bearing

(i) _____

(ii) _____

(iii) _____

(iv) _____

5 A pressure relief valve is found in:

(*a*) The thermostat ☐
(*b*) The petrol pump ☐
(*c*) The petrol tank ☐
(*d*) The oil pump ☐

6 Oil is detected in the water. The most likely reason is:

(*a*) Topping up with oil while it is raining ☐
(*b*) Leaking rocker-cover gasket ☐
(*c*) Blown cylinder-head gasket ☐
(*d*) Forgetting to replace the dipstick ☐

7 Which of the following could cause loss of compression:

(*a*) Wrong octane grade of petrol ☐
(*b*) Leak in exhaust manifold ☐
(*c*) Valve stuck open ☐
(*d*) Leak in inlet manifold ☐

8 When joining 'jump leads' between two negative-earthed batteries, where would you make the *first* connection:

(*a*) Positive of charged battery ☐
(*b*) Negative of charged battery ☐
(*c*) Positive of discharged battery ☐
(*d*) Negative of discharged battery ☐

9 One of these should be checked daily if the car is in regular use:

(*a*) Oil ☐
(*b*) Tyres ☐
(*c*) Battery ☐
(*d*) Water for windscreen washer ☐

10 Your car runs out of water while you are driving. Fortunately, you have a spare can of water in the boot. When filling, would you:

(*a*) Do nothing until the engine had cooled down ☐
(*b*) Pour the water in slowly with the engine running ☐
(*c*) Half fill the radiator and run the engine before completely filling ☐
(*d*) Pour the water in immediately so as to cool the engine quickly ☐

Check your answers from page 114 and enter here:

Total scored ☐ points

Time taken ☐ minutes

Now read the explanations of this test before continuing.

Explanations

1   (*a*) Ignition too far advanced will not give sluggishness at all speeds. Many years ago a driver had to advance or retard the ignition, according to the circumstances, by operating a lever on the steering column. It was usual to retard it when going uphill and advance it when going downhill. Nowadays this is taken care of automatically by the suction control attached to the distributor and by the centrifugal flyweights inside the contact-breaker assembly.

(*b*) Burning of the CB points cannot result from an error in the ignition timing, whether too far advanced or retarded, since their operation only provides (indirectly) for the spark at the plugs, whether this occurs early or late.

(*c*) Spitting in the carburettor (see explanation to question 6 (b) in Test 3) may be the result of a weak mixture, and might also occur from the ignition being too far retarded—but not too far advanced.

(*d*) Pinking, however, can certainly result from the ignition being too far advanced, for the reasons explained in question 6 (a), Test 3.

2   A 'variable jet' type of carburettor has a tapered needle which moves up or down according to the engine

revolutions or, as in the case of the SU carburettor, by suction. This carburettor has only one jet, situated at the base of the assembly, and the needle rises or falls into it. Due to the tapered contour of the needle, the jet orifice is enlarged or made smaller, as can be seen in this diagram:

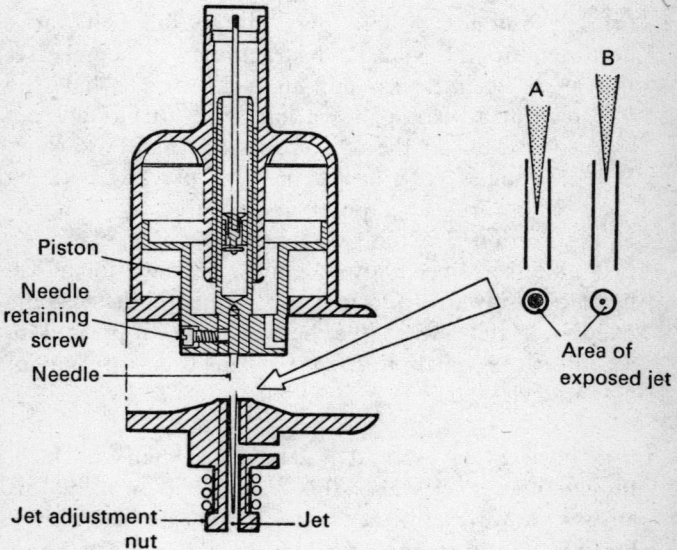

As the needle drops lower into the jet a smaller orifice is exposed, and less petrol can pass through the jet A. (The taper of the needle has been exaggerated in the diagram to make this more clear.) When the needle rises a larger orifice is exposed and more petrol can pass through B. The same effect as in A would be produced if the jet adjust adjusting nut (and hence the jet) were screwed upwards.

On no account should the position of the needle be altered, so only (*b*) and (*d*) are possible answers. Moving the jet upwards would obviously weaken the mixture by reducing the amount of petrol, so (*d*) is the correct answer.

3   (*a*) The amount of free play in the fan belt varies according to the maker's instructions—in some cases it may be as little as half an inch—but to have no free play at all would be wrong, since this would put excessive strain on the dynamo or alternator bearings. It is customary to measure the free play by pressing the belt inwards at a point about mid-way along its longest section. The total amount of free play, of course, is double this, since allowance must be made for movement both inwards and outwards; thus, if the maker's handbook states that the belt should be pressed in a quarter of an inch, this really means total free play of half an inch.

(*b*) The free play should not be more than one inch, though often it is less than this—about half an inch. This answer, however, is the most appropriate one, since the question asks *approximately* how much play there should be, and this answer is *about* an inch.

(*c*) This would be too much free play and would result in the fan belt slipping on the pulleys. This in turn would cause overheating of the water and under-charging of the battery.

(*d*) Three inches of free play would be so excessive that the fan belt would probably come off the pulleys altogether.

4 (i) If it is difficult to engage bottom gear while stationary the fault is likely to be that the engine is running too fast, and can be remedied simply by altering the setting of the throttle stop screw. There are, of course, other, more serious causes of this, such as wear on the pinions of bottom gear, or clutch drag, resulting from (*d*). If difficulty is found in engaging bottom while stationary and the engine is *not* running too fast, there are two ways of overcoming it on the spot, though the fault should then be rectified mechanically. One way is to engage second gear and *immediately* transfer the gear lever to the bottom gear position. Another way, even quicker, is merely to touch the synchromesh unit of second gear (the point at which slight resistance is felt before the gear is actually engaged) and then immediately switch into bottom gear.

(ii) If the front wheels are out of balance, this symptom —often called 'wheel wobble'—would manifest itself at certain speeds. It may be found that at precisely 40 mph, for example, the vibration is set up. Normality can be restored in one of two ways: either by increasing the speed until the vibration ceases, or by decreasing the speed to below that at which the vibration begins. Neither method is entirely satisfactory: the second can unduly delay you on a journey of some urgency, while the first method is hardly recommended since, in the process of increasing the speed to reach a smooth pitch, the wobble can become alarmingly increased. The only satisfactory solution is to have the wheels balanced as soon as possible. There are many garages which advertise this service, and it is not costly. Lead weights are attached to the wheel rims to maintain true rotation at all speeds.

(iii) If road speed does not pick up proportionately

with engine speed (particularly when going uphill) it is a sign that the clutch is slipping. The only item that could cause this is (*b*)—no free play in the clutch pedal, meaning that the clutch plate is not fully pressed home against the flywheel.

(iv) If the clutch 'whines' when the pedal is depressed it is likely that the clutch release bearing is worn, but the only item mentioned that could also cause it is a dry spigot bearing. This is at the centre of the flywheel and supports the front end of the clutch shaft.

5 The most common type of oil pump (*d*), submerged in the oil in the sump, is the gear type, which simply consists of two gear wheels meshed with each other. The teeth are cut wide and in such a way that pockets are formed between them and the walls of the pump casing, as shown below.

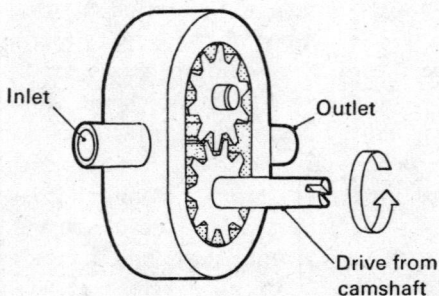

Inlet

Outlet

Drive from camshaft

One of the gears is mounted on a shaft which is driven from the camshaft, while the other is free to rotate on its stub axle. Oil enters the pump through the inlet and before being able to leave through the outlet has to make its way round the teeth of the gears. When oil is passed through gear wheels it builds up a pressure (just like water passing through a water-mill) and the pressure varies according to the speed of the gears. (This is why a gearbox should never be over-filled with oil; if this were done a pressure would build up inside the gearbox, which could lead to damage and leakage.) The oil then leaves the pump under pressure.

If excessive pressure were allowed to build up (which would happen as the engine speed increased) damage would be done to the bearings and seals. For this reason a pressure relief valve is incorporated in the pump. This is simply a spring-loaded metal ball which is pushed off its seating when a predetermined pressure is reached, so that oil in excess of that pressure goes straight through the pump and not round the gears.

6 If oil has entered the water, the two must have mixed somewhere in the cooling system.

(*a*) & (*b*) If a lot of water found its way into the sump oil, it might dilute the oil; but the infinitesimal amount that would enter while topping up in rain, or by forgetting to replace the dipstick, would be of negligible account.

(*b*) A leaking rocker-cover gasket would allow oil to escape from the overhead valve mechanism, resulting in a messy engine and, of course, excessive oil consumption through wastage.

(*c*) The cylinder-head gasket, however, has to be an air-tight, oil-tight and *water-tight* seal. If it were blown oil would assuredly mix with the water and be detected in the coolant.

7 Compression is dependent on many things, such as piston rings not worn, stuck or broken: valves operating correctly; cylinder-head gasket not leaking; cylinders not worn; cylinder-head nuts tight.

(*c*) The piston, on its compression stroke, must be as air-tight in the cylinder as possible; anything which could affect this would reduce compression. Obviously, then, (*c*) is the answer. If either valve did not fully close for any reason at all, compression must suffer, as *both* valves must be *fully* closed on the compression stroke. This is why correct valve clearance should be maintained. A valve can fail to close properly for a variety of reasons, such as deposit on the valve (sometimes caused, especially on the inlet valve, by excessive lead additive in the petrol).

(*a*) Grade of petrol (octane rating) cannot influence compression, though it can, of course, influence power and cause pinking if the octane grade is too low.

(*b*) & (*d*) As both inlet and exhaust valves are closed on the compression stroke it would be immaterial whether there was a leak in either the exhaust manifold or the inlet manifold.

8 Jump leads are useful for starting the engine when the battery is flat, provided another car is available, but it is very important to observe certain rules when connecting them, as a mistake could not only damage the electrical components, but cause serious injury as well. Unless precautions are taken there is always a risk of battery explosion or injury to the eyes as acid squirts out of the battery vents.

Follow the procedure for connecting the jump leads as given in (*a*), then proceed like this:

1. Although the two vehicles must be close enough for the jump leads to reach to the batteries, on no account must they touch each other.

2. Remove the filler caps from *both* batteries and cover the open vents with cloths. If the batteries have vent balls in the cells, remove these (with a cloth —*not* with the fingers!).

3. Connect one lead to the positive terminal post of the charged battery.

4. Connect the other end of this lead to the positive terminal post of the discharged battery.

5. Connect one end of the other lead to the negative terminal post of the charged battery.

6. Connect the other end of this lead to the EARTH STRAP (not the terminal post) of the discharged battery. Stand well clear when making this final connection.

7. Start the engine of the car that has the booster battery before trying to start the other engine.

(The sequence should be reversed once the other engine has started.)

Any other sequence, as has been stated, could lead to damage or personal injury. Therefore, (*b*), (*c*) and (*d*) must all be considered as wrong answers.

9 (*a*) The level of the oil in the sump should never be taken for granted, and it should be checked every day if the car is in regular use. Throughout the life of the engine, oil consumption will tend to increase, albeit on such a gradual scale that only over a long period would it become noticeable. Admittedly, with regular use a driver gets to know approximately how many miles he can expect to cover before the oil needs topping up; nevertheless he should check daily, as leaks can occur at any time. Although there is no advantage (indeed many disadvantages) in *over*-filling, the oil level should never be allowed to drop too low, but should be maintained at the highest point marked on the dipstick.

(*b*), (*c*) and (*d*) These should be checked every week.

10 (*d*) This is the worst answer. Pouring cold water quickly on to boiling water can cause serious damage (and serious injury through scalding). Metal expands under heat, and all metal parts in the cooling system—the radiator core, the pistons, the cylinders, combustion chambers, cylinder-head, and even the thermostat—will be cooled suddenly, causing contraction. This contraction must be allowed to take place gradually, and the most effective way of achieving this is to let the parts cool down *in their own time*.

(*a*) Thus, (*a*) is the only completely satisfactory answer.

If circumstances simply do not allow for natural cooling, the next best thing is to wait for a while for some cooling to take place and then follow the procedure in (*b*)—pour the water in *slowly* while the engine is running. The slow pouring will encourage more gradual contraction of the metal, and having the engine running will keep the water circulating through the action of the pump.

Test 5

1 A sympton indicating that the brakes need bleeding is:

   (*a*) Brakes pulling to one side ☐
   (*b*) 'Spongy' feeling in brake pedal ☐
   (*c*) Brakes not fully pulling off ☐
   (*d*) Wheels lock when brakes are used ☐

2 The diagram below shows the valves in a typical four-cylindered engine. Assuming that No. 1 valve is open, is No. 8 valve:

   (*a*) Fully open ☐
   (*b*) Fully closed ☐
   (*c*) Just opening ☐
   (*d*) Just closing ☐

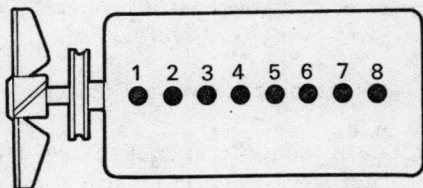

3 Clutch slip can be diagnosed from:

   (*a*) Difficulty in changing gear ☐
   (*b*) Road speed not increasing in proportion with engine speed ☐
   (*c*) Engine not idling correctly ☐
   (*d*) Too much play in the clutch pedal ☐

4 At what point in the diagram below would you adjust the fan belt:

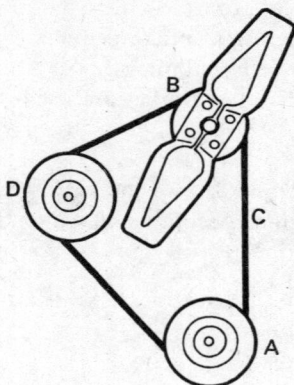

5 If a headlight went out while driving, which would you suspect:

(*a*) Broken bulb

(*b*) Bad earth connection to battery

(*c*) Broken fuse

(*d*) Fault in the charging system

6 Here are four pairs of statements. In only *one* pair are *both* statements correct:

(*a*) Rain water is an ideal coolant.
Electric current flows from positive to negative.

(*b*) A thermostat prevents overheating.
Jumping out of gear can be caused by a weak selector spring.

(*c*) The thermostat should be removed in the summer.
When draining the radiator the heater should be in the 'hot' position. ☐

(*d*) Sparking plugs should be as tight as possible so as not to lose compression.
The radiator of a VW 'Beetle' is at the rear. ☐

7 Which items do you associate with (i) Brakes; (ii) Petrol system; (iii) Ignition system; (iv) Starter motor.

(*a*) Needle valve
(*b*) Commutator
(*c*) Pressure relief valve
(*d*) Micrometer adjustment
(*e*) Master cylinder
(*f*) Tie rod

(i) _____

(ii) _____

(iii) _____

(iv) _____

8 When the front wheels are turned by the steering wheel one wheel turns more than the other. This is because one wheel describes a smaller turning circle than the other.
This is known as the '_____Principle'.

9 Petrol is not reaching the carburettor, though it is leaving the pump. Could the reason be:

(*a*) Leaking diaphragm in pump ☐
(*b*) Outlet valve of pump stuck closed ☐
(*c*) Blocked petrol pipe ☐
(*d*) Blocked filter in petrol pump ☐

10 The engine refuses to start and is not firing. A test shows that there is a good spark from the HT lead coming from the coil. The fault could be one of these:

(*a*) Dirty CB points ☐
(*b*) Broken plug lead ☐
(*c*) Worn carbon brush in distributor ☐
(*d*) Bad connection in the primary circuit ☐

Check your answers from page 114 and enter here:

Total scored ☐ points

Time taken ☐ minutes

Now read the explanations of this test before continuing.

Explanations

1 (*a*) If the brakes pull to one side there may be oil or water in one or more of the brake drums (or discs). This often happens after driving through flood water, and it can usually be cured by driving for a while using the brake and accelerator pedals together. Other things, such as wear in the suspension, could cause pulling to one side, but the symptom would not indicate that the brakes require bleeding.

(*b*) If the brake pedal travels a long way down before the brakes take effect, and efficiency can be restored by 'pumping' the pedal, this is a sign that there is air in the hydraulic system and that the brakes need bleeding to exclude the air (see question 10 in Test 1). A 'spongy' feeling in the pedal indicates the same fault.

(*c*) The pull-off springs are responsible for separating the brake shoes from the drums when the pedal is released.

(*d*) If a brake drum or disc is distorted or a wheel bearing is loose, the brakes might grip hard even when the pedal is pressed lightly.

2 In order to avoid having eight separate pipes feeding, and then extracting the burnt gases from the combustion chambers, 'manifolds' are used. Manifolds can serve

more than one valve at a time because some of the valves are arranged in pairs. In a 'typical' four-cylindered engine they are paired as follows:

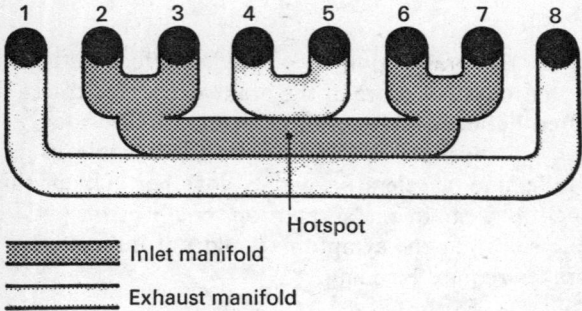

Hotspot

Inlet manifold

Exhaust manifold

No. 1 piston must be on its exhaust stroke, since its exhaust valve is open. No. 1 piston is paired with No. 4 piston, which is on its compression stroke (see explanation to question 3, Test 2). Since, on the compression stroke, *both* valves are closed, it follows that valves Nos. 7 and 8 are *both* closed.

3 Clutch 'slip' means that although the clutch pedal is completely up, the clutch plate is not rotating as one with the flywheel—the friction linings are slipping against each other.

This may be due to many reasons, such as oil on the linings.

(*d*) But would certainly not be due to too much play in

the pedal, which would have the opposite effect, causing clutch drag.

(*a*) would also be the result of clutch drag (if, indeed, the fault lay in the clutch, and not in the gearbox).

(*c*) A slipping clutch would have no effect at all on the idling speed of the engine (*c*). (Try the mixture control screw on the carburettor!)

4 The adjustment would be made at D, that is, at the dynamo or alternator.

A and B are the crankshaft and fan pulleys respectively and, of course, no adjustment is possible at them.

C is merely a mid-way point along one length of the fan belt.

To adjust the tension of the fan belt, proceed in this way:

1. Loosen the two mounting bolts of the dynamo or alternator;
2. Loosen the *two* bolts that secure the slotted bracket.

Having set the dynamo or alternator in the required position, tighten the bolts in this order:

1. Front mounting bolt of dynamo or alternator;
2. Slotted bracket to alternator bolt;
3. Rear mounting bolt of dynamo or alternator;
4. Bolt securing slotted bracket to engine.

If using a lever to move the alternator, damage can be done by levering at the rear end. *Always* lever the front end.

5 (*c*) As *both* headlights, if protected by a fuse at all, are protected by the same one, they would both fail if the fuse broke.

(*b*) & (*d*) Similarly, a fault in either the charging system or a battery connection would affect both headlights.

(*a*) If only one light fails it must be a fault connected with that light, such as a loose connection, a broken lead, a bad earth, or *a broken bulb*, which is the correct answer.

6 (*a*) Rain water is an ideal coolant, and some motorists keep a rain butt in the garden to collect it. It is important not to use a metal container for this purpose, and to filter the water before using it in the radiator.

Current flows from positive to negative, even if the positive terminal of the battery is earthed.

(*b*) A thermostat does not prevent overheating. (An answer to a later question divulges its true purpose.)

The selector spring forces a retaining ball into a recess on the selector rod, preventing the rod from moving and thus disengaging the gear. A weak spring could be overcome, causing the rod to move and the gear to jump out.

(*c*) There is no need to remove the thermostat in the summer since, being a heat-operated valve, it will remain open when the *water* temperature reaches a certain level, whatever the outside temperature may be. If a thermostat were stuck in the closed position, causing overheating, it would be advisable to remove it *in summer or winter* until a new one could be fitted. No damage would be done while running the engine without it, though in the winter you might have to be more patient (the reason will be given in a later explanation).

When draining the radiator it is advisable to have the heater in the 'hot' position to reduce the risk of an air-lock.

(*d*) It is a mistake to fit sparking plugs as tightly as possible. Around the thread of the sparking plug there is a gasket which ensures an air-tight fit so that there is no loss of compression. When fitting a plug always make sure that this gasket (or washer) is in position. Over-tightening could damage the gasket—and make it difficult to remove the plug later.

The VW 'Beetle' has an air-cooled engine (which *is* at the rear); therefore it has no radiator.

7 (i) The master cylinder (*e*) is the only item which is associated with the brakes. Fluid from the reservoir enters the master cylinder and pressure on the pedal activates a spring-loaded piston in the cylinder, forcing the fluid along the pipe-lines to the wheel cylinders.

(ii) The needle valve (*a*) controls the flow of petrol into the float chamber of the carburettor. When the float drops as the level of petrol falls, the needle valve opens and allows more petrol to enter. The float then rises on the level of the petrol and closes the valve, cutting off further supply of petrol. The diagram below shows the principle of this:

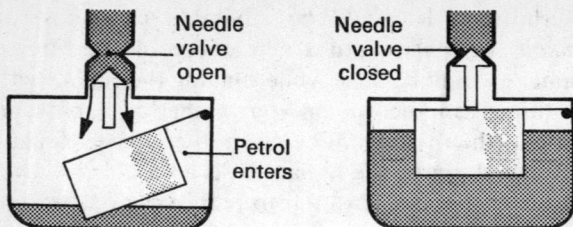

Needle valve open — Petrol enters

Needle valve closed

Thus the needle valve maintains a constant level of petrol in the float chamber and prevents it from over-filling.

(iii) Some distributors are fitted with a micrometer adjustment (sometimes called a 'vernier control'). This very useful attachment enables the ignition to be advanced or retarded within very fine limits.

(iv) The starter motor contains an armature, the spindle of which is formed into a commutator. The carbon brushes, bearing on the commutator, pass current from the battery, causing rotation of the spindle.

Neither of the remaining items are associated. A pressure relief valve is found in the oil pump and a tie rod is part of the steering linkage.

8 When the front wheels are turned by the steering wheel the outer wheel has to describe a larger turning circle than the inner wheel, according to which way they are turned (see below).

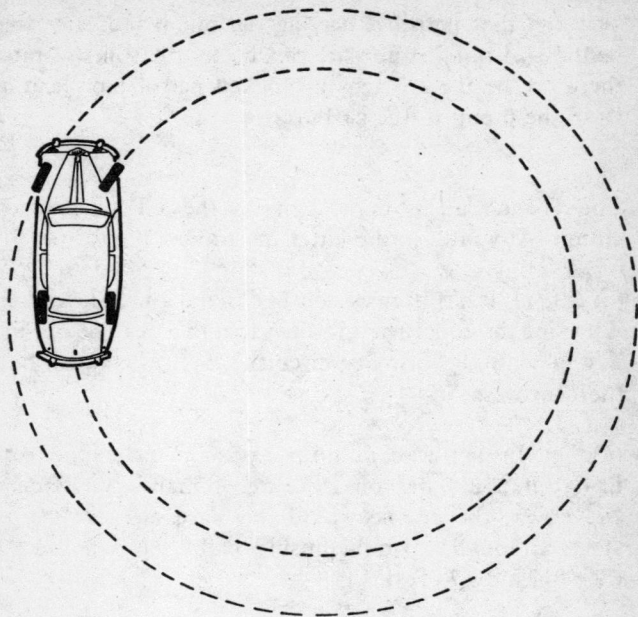

Each of the front wheels is connected to the track rod by a steering arm, as shown below. These arms are set at an angle so that if a line were taken through each and continued to the rear the two lines would meet at a point mid-way across the rear of the car. This is known as the 'Ackerman' Principle.

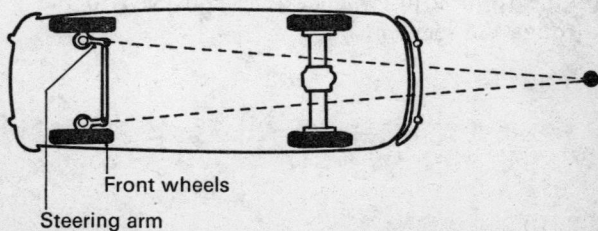

Front wheels

Steering arm

9 The fact that petrol is leaving the pump indicates that neither (*a*) nor (*b*) nor (*d*) can be the reason. (*c*) must therefore be the answer—a blocked petrol pipe leading from the pump to the carburettor.

10 The HT circuit is dependent on the LT or primary circuit. Any fault in the latter must affect the former.

(*a*) & (*d*) If it has been established that a good HT current is leaving the coil, then it follows that there can be nothing wrong with the primary circuit, which eliminates both these answers.

(*b*) One broken lead would not prevent the engine from firing; it could fire on the three remaining cylinders. Moreover, the engine would not necessarily refuse to start, although it would misfire badly when it did so. (See question 7, Test 2.)

(*c*) The obvious answer is that the HT current, though leaving the coil, is not reaching the plugs. This could be for a variety of reasons: dirty segments in the distributor; all plugs faulty; dirty plugs. But the only item listed is 'worn carbon brush in distributor', and that is the answer here. The object of this small block of carbon is to transfer the HT current from the coil lead to the top of the rotor arm, whence it is conveyed to the plugs through the segments.

Test 6

1 The HT spark occurs when the CB points are:

    (*a*) Fully open ☐
    (*b*) Fully closed ☐
    (*c*) Just beginning to open ☐
    (*d*) Just beginning to close ☐

2 The best way to clear a blocked jet is to:

    (*a*) Blow through it ☐
    (*b*) Push a thin piece of wire through it ☐
    (*c*) Wash it in petrol ☐
    (*d*) Hold it under a running tap ☐

3 Which item or items do you associate with (i) Steering,
  (ii) Starter motor, (iii) Gearbox, (iv) Differential:

    (*a*) Layshaft   (*f*) Hypoid bevel gear
    (*b*) Rack and pinion   (*g*) Mainshaft
    (*c*) Crown wheel and pinion   (*h*) Track rod end
    (*d*) Castor angle   (*i*) Bendix pinion
    (*e*) Quickthread   (*j*) Camber angle

(i) _____

(ii) _____

(iii) _____

(iv) _____

4 What is the ratio between pinions A and C in the diagram below:

    (*a*) 2:1 ☐
    (*b*) 4:1 ☐
    (*c*) 1:1 ☐
    (*d*) 5:1 ☐

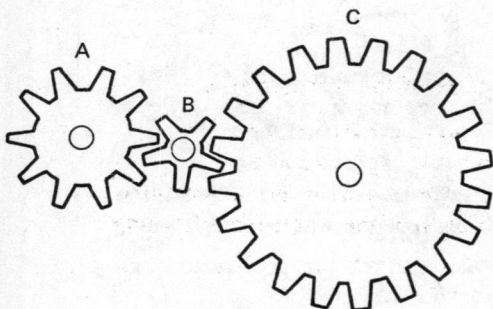

5 The front tyres are wearing very quickly, and examination shows that wear is mainly taking place on the edges, which look 'feathered'. Would you suspect:

    (*a*) Tyres under-inflated ☐
    (*b*) Tyres over-inflated ☐
    (*c*) Incorrect camber angle ☐
    (*d*) Wrong toe-in ☐

6 Unusually low pressure shown on an oil gauge could indicate:

    (*a*) Insufficient oil in sump ☐
    (*b*) Oil too thick ☐
    (*c*) Worn big-end bearings ☐
    (*d*) No oil in sump ☐

7 If the headlights dim when decelerating, which of these would you suspect:

    (*a*) Bulb(s) need replacing ☐
    (*b*) Loose fan blade ☐
    (*c*) Loose fan belt ☐
    (*d*) Broken fuse ☐

8 The object of the thermostat is:

    (*a*) To prevent overheating. ☐
    (*b*) To assist rapid warm-up ☐
    (*c*) To prevent a build-up of pressure ☐
    (*b*) To prevent the water from freezing ☐

9 Numbering the valves from front to rear on a typical four-cylindered engine, which would be the exhaust valves:

    (*a*) 1 4 5 8 ☐
    (*b*) 1 3 6 8 ☐
    (*c*) 2 5 6 8 ☐
    (*b*) 1 4 6 8 ☐

10 Which of these do you associate with the spigot bearing:

    (*a*) Differential ☐
    (*b*) Wheel ☐
    (*c*) Flywheel ☐
    (*d*) Universal joint ☐

Check your answers from page 115 and enter here:

Total scored ☐ points

Time taken ☐ minutes

Now read the explanations of this test before continuing.

Explanations

1 Briefly, the theory of converting the low tension output of the battery into the high tension necessary to jump the gap at the plug points is this: LT current is passed through the windings of a coil which is wound round a soft iron core. This magnetizes the iron core, producing an 'electro-magnet'. Around this is wound another coil of wire, which is the 'secondary' winding.

If the LT current is cut off—as it is every time the CB points open—the magnetic field collapses, cutting through the windings of the secondary coil. At the instant of collapse HT current is momentarily induced into the secondary coil.

(*c*) Therefore the spark occurs at the first moment of opening.

(*a*) When the points are fully open no HT current is flowing.

(*d*) Nor is the current flowing when they are beginning to close.

(*b*) When they are fully closed LT current is flowing through them and returning to earth, but no HT current will be induced until the next time they *just begin* to open.

2 (*a*) The *only* acceptable way to clear a blocked jet is to blow through it. The jet meters out petrol in the exact quantity required and the small hole which allows for this is precisely measured.

(*b*) Any method that tends to enlarge this hole must be avoided, and the worst possible thing to do is to push a piece of wire through it.

(*c*) To wash it in petrol would do no harm, but it would not necessarily clear the blockage; after all, the jet is immersed in petrol all the time, but still dirt managed to find its way into it.

(*d*) Water is the last thing to bring into contact with petrol. Admittedly, if the jet were thoroughly dried afterwards no harm would be done, but it would be difficult to run water through such a tiny hole with enough pressure to clear a blockage.

3 (i) (*b*) Various methods are used to convert the rotary motion of the steering column into the lateral movement of the front wheels, and the gearing which allows for this is housed in the steering box at the base of the steering column. One of the most common types of conversion is the 'rack and pinion', the principle being that rotation of the steering column causes the drop arm to swing to and fro, which in turn moves the steering arm. The steering arm swivels the front wheel on its stub axle. Other types of steering gear are: cam-and-roller, cam-and-peg, worm-and-nut, worm-and-peg and recirculating-ball.

(*d*) The advantage of fitting a castor to the leg of a heavy piece of furniture is that the weight of the furniture is taken by the leg but, due to the crook in the castor, the point of contact between the castor wheel and the floor is not the same as the axis through the leg. In fact, the wheel of the castor is trailing behind the weight:

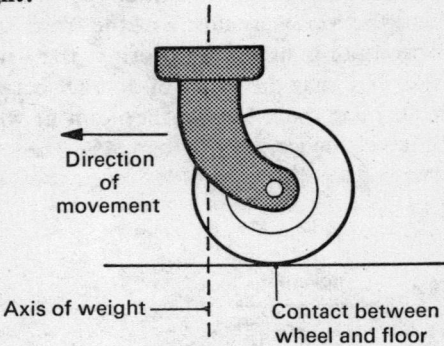

Direction of movement

Axis of weight ——— Contact between wheel and floor

As the furniture is turned the castor will swivel round so as to follow behind the weight. The result of this is that it is very much easier to push the furniture. A similar result is produced by the front fork of a bicycle, which is cranked:

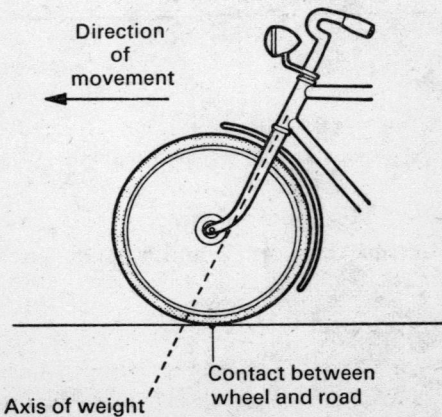

Direction of movement

Contact between wheel and road

Axis of weight

This makes steering the bicycle much easier than in the days of the old 'penny-farthing', which had a vertical front fork. The steering was very heavy when the handlebars were turned or straightened after turning.

This 'castor action' is a feature of the front wheels of a car. To promote lightness of steering, the wheels are set in such a way that the point of contact between the tyres and the road trails behind the point at which the weight of the vehicle strikes the road:

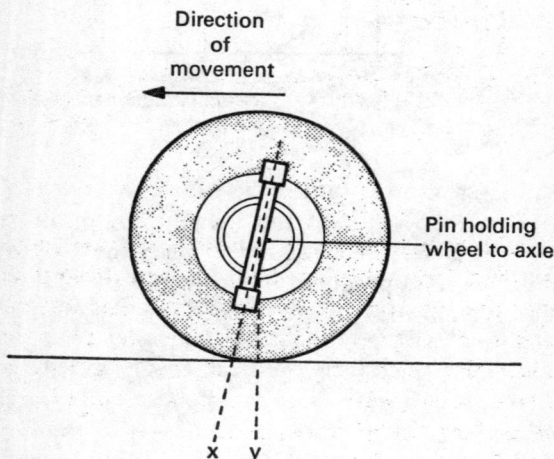

Direction
of
movement

Pin holding
wheel to axle

x y

The difference between x and y is the 'castor angle'.

(*h*) Continuing the story of the 'geometry' of the steering: it is also necessary for the front wheels not to be set parallel with each other. They should be slightly closer at the front than at the rear:

The wheels tend to splay outwards in travel, and this is allowed for by having them inclined inwards at the front. The diagram above exaggerates this inclination, which is actually very slight—usually only one sixteenth to one eighth of an inch. Without 'toe-in', as it is called, the tyres would wear more rapidly and more unevenly. (See explanation of question 5.)

The front wheels are connected to each other by the track rod, the ends of which ('track rod ends') are adjustable so that the wheels can be moved slightly in or out in relationship to each other. (In some cases, where radial tyres are fitted, no toe-in is recommended.)

(*j*) A front wheel does not stand absolutely vertical, but is inclined slightly outwards at the top, though this inclination is not always discernible with the naked eye. (It is usually quite pronounced on sports cars.) In motion the wheel tends to assume the vertical position, and this is allowed for by the camber angle:

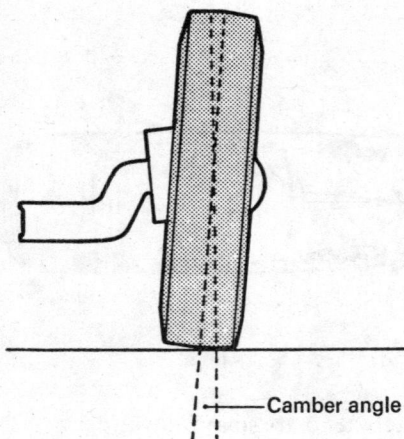

Camber angle

(ii) (*e*) The starter motor has a shaft extending from it which is placed alongside the starter ring on the fly-wheel. Part of this shaft forms a wide spiral, known as the 'quickthread'. Fitting over the quickthread is a loose-fitting pinion, known as the 'bendix pinion.' Actuation of the motor by passing current through it when the starter is operated makes the quickthread rotate and 'throw out' the pinion, causing the pinion to move along the shaft and engage with the teeth of the starter ring:

Starter pinion not engaged

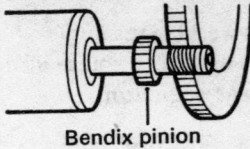

Bendix pinion

Starter pinion engaged with flywheel

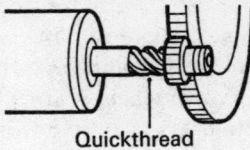

Quickthread

(iii) The diagram below shows some of the components of a gearbox. The layshaft is driven from the clutch shaft through the constant mesh pinions, which reduce the speed of the layshaft as compared with the crankshaft. A difference in the speeds between the layshaft and mainshaft is brought about by pinions of various sizes on one shaft being turned by those on the other:

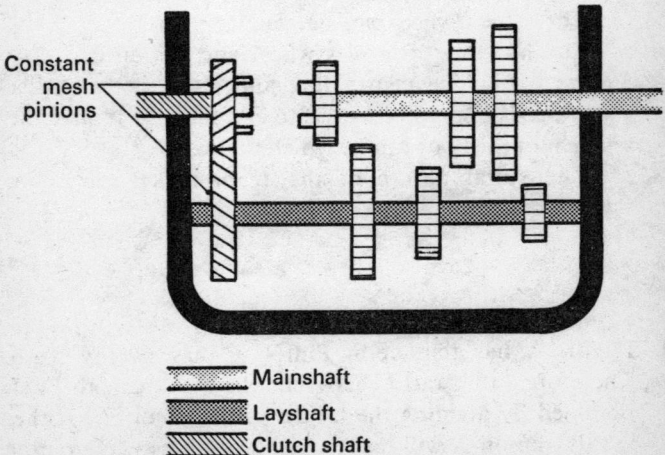

Constant mesh pinions

Mainshaft
Layshaft
Clutch shaft

(iv) The differential has three functions:

To transfer the drive at right angles.
To allow the rear wheels to rotate at different speeds.
To give a final gear reduction.

The rear end of the propeller shaft is supported in a bearing and forms a spiral bevel pinion which drives the crown wheel. Because there are more teeth on the crown wheel than on the pinion there is a final reduction in the speed of the rear wheels as compared with the speed of the crankshaft. The crown wheel is at right angles to the pinion, and hence transfers the drive from the propeller shaft to the back axle at right angles. The crown wheel carries the differential assembly, which allows the two half-shafts to rotate at different speeds when turning corners.

(*f*) The teeth on the crown wheel and pinion in the case of hypoid bevel gears are cut in a spiral shape, which allows for three things:

The crown wheel can be smaller.
The meshing of crown wheel and pinion can take place below the centre line and thus the propeller shaft can be set lower, so as to eliminate or reduce the height of the floor tunnel which houses it.
The spiral nature of the teeth makes the drive much quieter.

4 Pinion A has ten teeth. Pinion C has twenty teeth. Therefore, the ratio between them is exactly 2:1, obtained by dividing the larger by the smaller. In other words, pinion A will make two revolutions while pinion

C makes one. Notice that the number of teeth on the intervening pinion B does not in any way alter the ratio of the other two (I gave it five because that number is divisible into the number on the other pinions). All it influences is the direction of rotation. If A and C were meshed together they would rotate in opposite directions, but by interposing pinion B they both rotate in the same direction.

Knowledge of gear ratios, direction of rotation, and the influence of interposed pinions is necessary when dealing with geared components, such as the gearbox and the timing mechanism. The principle outlined above is put into practice when reverse gear is engaged.

5 Wear on the front tyres can give valuable information about the condition of the steering, among other things.

(a) Tyres that are worn along the outsides indicate that they have been under-inflated:

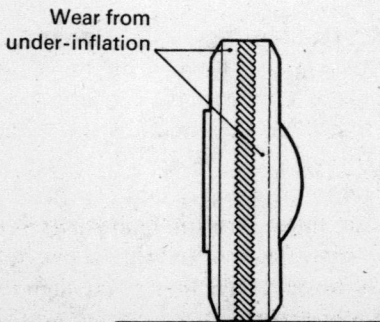

Wear from
under-inflation

(*b*) If the crown of the tyre is worn, while the outside edges are in good condition, it implies that the tyres have been over-inflated:

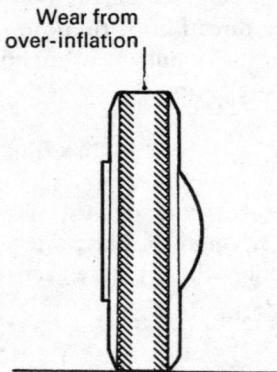

Wear from
over-inflation

(*c*) A tyre worn unevenly on one side only indicates something wrong with the steering geometry.

(*d*) If the toe-in is wrong the tyre will have a 'feathered' appearance along its edges.

6 There is no such thing as 'normal' oil pressure, but by continually driving a car fitted with an oil gauge a driver gets to know what the *usual* pressure should be for that particular car when the engine is warmed up.

(*a*) Insufficient oil in the sump would not affect pressure (except when cornering) since the inlet for the oil pump is situated in the lowest part of the sump; provided there is oil in the sump it would have to pass through the pump to reach the main oil gallery.

(*b*) If the oil were too thick it would register a higher pressure.

(*c*) 'Unusually low' oil pressure could indicate worn bearings—either main bearings or big-end bearings.

(*d*) Obviously, if there were no oil in the sump there would be a zero reading on the gauge.

7 (*d*) A broken fuse would certainly not be the reason for the headlights dimming under deceleration. They would not light at all!

(*a*) The bulbs themselves would not be suspect for two reasons: first, because it is unlikely that both bulbs would be faulty at the same time, but mainly because they have already shown their efficiency under acceleration.

(*b*) So long as the fan belt is turning the generator correctly it would not matter if there were a loose fan *blade* (though this should be rectified before serious damage to the radiator results).

(*c*) If, however, the fan belt were loose it would not turn the generator at sufficient speed, especially when decelerating.
   The most usual reason for headlights dimming is that the battery is not fully charged and, of course, if the generator is not giving its full output (especially with the headlights on, which would take more out of it than would otherwise be the case) the battery would *not* be fully charged.

8 The explanation of question 4 in Test 3 showed how the water circulates through the cooling system by convection. But for this to happen the water must be hot; once the heat from the engine has been conducted into the water, circulation will take place. The internal combustion engine is only completely efficient when it is warmed up, the ideal running temperature being about 180 degrees fahrenheit. Therefore, when starting from cold it is essential that this operating temperature is reached as quickly as possible, and this is where the thermostat comes into the story. The thermostat is a heat-operated valve, shown in the diagram below:

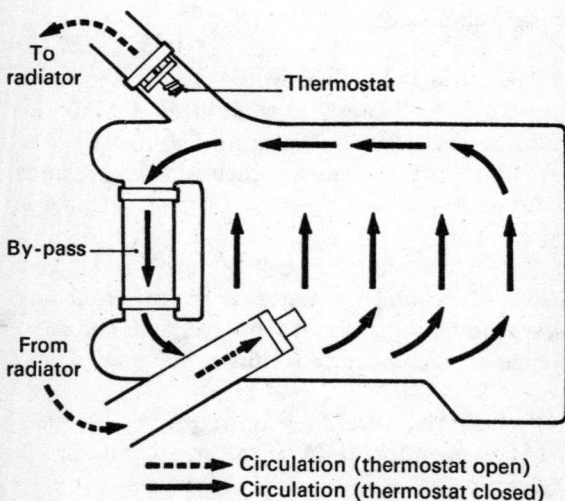

To radiator

Thermostat

By-pass

From radiator

- - - → Circulation (thermostat open)
——→ Circulation (thermostat closed)

_____Circulation (thermostat open)

_____Circulation (thermostat closed)

When the water is cold the valve is closed, and this prevents the water rising from the cylinder block and entering the header tank of the radiator. If the water can be held back from the radiator it will not become even more cooled by passing through the radiator. A by-pass brings the warmed water back to the bottom of the engine, and as soon as the hot water reaches a predetermined temperature the thermostat valve opens, allowing the water thereafter to circulate through the radiator.

Should the temperature drop, the thermostat will close, or partially close, to stop or restrict further circulation through the radiator until maximum efficient temperature is again reached.

(*b*) Thus the object of the thermostat is to ensure rapid warming up of the engine.

(*a*) To prevent overheating is not its object.

(*c*) The thermostat does not prevent a build-up of pressure.

(*d*) Nor can it prevent the water from freezing. If the temperature falls below freezing-point, then the water is liable to freeze with or without the inclusion of the thermostat.

9　The diagram of the valves in question 2 of Test 5 shows that the exhaust valves on a typical four-cylindered engine are 1, 4, 5 and 8. As was explained, in order to avoid a multiplicity of pipes leading to the valves, manifolds are used, which enable some of the valves to be paired together. Valves 2 and 3 (inlet) are paired; valves 4 and 5 (exhaust) are paired; and valves 6 and 7 (inlet) are paired.

10 The spigot bearing is in the flywheel and supports the front end of the clutch shaft:

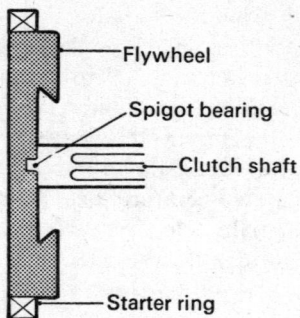

Test 7

1 After replacing an old air cleaner element with a new one it may be necessary to alter:

   (*a*) The CB points ☐
   (*b*) The mixture control screw ☐
   (*c*) The plug gap ☐
   (*d*) The ignition timing ☐

2 The firing order can *always* be ascertained from *one* of the following:

   (*a*) Watching the valve movements ☐
   (*b*) Inspecting the plug leads at the distributor and plugs ☐
   (*c*) Finding the direction of rotation of the rotor arm ☐
   (*d*) Removing the plugs and watching the sparks ☐

3 Clutch drag means that when the pedal is fully pressed the clutch plate does not come fully away from the flywheel. This can be caused by:

   (*a*) Weak clutch springs ☐
   (*b*) Driving with the foot over the clutch pedal ☐
   (*c*) Insufficient play in clutch pedal ☐
   (*d*) Too much play in clutch pedal ☐

4 Would excessively high oil pressure be most likely to indicate:

   (*a*) Oil too thin ☐
   (*b*) Too much oil in sump ☐
   (*c*) Pressure relief valve stuck ☐
   (*d*) Worn bearings ☐

5 Could worn cylinders cause:

   (*a*) Black smoke but no loss of power ☐
   (*b*) White smoke and loss of power ☐
   (*c*) Blue smoke and loss of power ☐
   (*d*) Black smoke and loss of power ☐

6 Mark these statements as TRUE or FALSE:

   (*a*) An arrow on the rotor arm always indicates the direction of rotation.   TRUE/FALSE
   (*b*) If the rotor arm rotates clockwise the distributor should also be rotated clockwise to retard the ignition.   TRUE/FALSE
   (*c*) The rotor arm transfers LT current to the plugs through the segments.   TRUE/FALSE
   (*d*) A hair-line crack in a distributor cap can cause misfiring.   TRUE/FALSE

7 While driving at night the headlights flicker on and off. The reason might be:

   (*a*) Battery not fully charged ☐
   (*b*) Loose fuse ☐
   (*c*) Loose fan belt ☐
   (*d*) Faulty bulbs ☐

8 When the steering wheel is fully turned the road wheels turn further in one direction than the other. To rectify this:

(*a*) Change the position of the steering wheel ☐
(*b*) Adjust the track rod ends ☐
(*c*) Adjust the position of the drop arm ☐
(*d*) Tighten the wheel bearings ☐

9 No petrol is getting into the float chamber, even though it is leaving the inlet pipe to the carburettor. Could this be due to:

(*a*) Outlet valve in pump stuck closed ☐
(*b*) A punctured float ☐
(*c*) A blocked jet ☐
(*d*) Dirt in the needle valve ☐

10 You can start the engine if you have lost the ignition key (provided the starter button is separate from the ignition switch or there is a solenoid button in the starting system) by connecting a length of wire:

(*a*) From the unearthed battery terminal to the CB terminal on the coil ☐
(*b*) From the earthed battery terminal to the CB terminal on the coil ☐
(*c*) From the earthed battery terminal to the SW terminal on the coil ☐
(*d*) From the unearthed battery terminal to the SW terminal on the coil ☐

Check your answers from page 115 and enter here:

Total scored ☐ points

Time taken ☐ minutes

Now read the explanations of this test before continuing.

Explanations

1 (*a*) The air cleaner element influences the ratio between air and petrol (which is vital to the fuel system), and since the fuel system is quite separate from the electrical system, it could not affect the CB points.

(*b*) The old air cleaner element was probably replaced because it was choked up with dirt and sludge. This impediment to the flow of air through it was reducing the volume of air as compared with the mixture of petrol and air essential to the smooth running of the engine. A new element will allow more air to pass through, and it may be necessary to alter the setting of the mixture control screw to compensate for this.

(*c*) The spark between the electrodes of the sparking plugs is governed by the ignition system, and could not be affected by the mixture.

(*d*) The ignition timing determines the exact moment at which the mixture—already arranged for in the fuel system—is ignited. Therefore it can in no way influence the running of the engine, whether using an old air cleaner element or a new one.

2 The firing order can be ascertained by finding the direction of rotation of the rotor arm (*c*) *and* by tracing the plug leads from the distributor to the plugs (*b*), *but neither one by itself is conclusive evidence*. Indeed, there is even a fallacy involved when both factors are considered, since it is assumed that the plug leads are connected in the correct order, whereas firing-order may be required to check that the leads *are* connected correctly!

(*d*) Removing the plugs and watching the sparks would undoubtedly establish the firing order—but there may be no sparks to watch! The battery may be flat, or there may be a fault in the ignition system which prevents the sparks from occurring.

The question clearly asks for an infallible way of finding the firing-order and makes no provision for everything else being in satisfactory condition.

(*a*) But the valves will operate, whether the battery is flat or not, and watching them is the one sure method of establishing the firing-order. The engine is turned until No. 1 valve (exhaust) opened. Then, watching valves 4, 5 and 8 (the remaining exhaust valves) the next one to open is the next in firing-order. Now watching the remaining two valves would establish the sequence of the two remaining cylinders. This would give the order in which the exhaust strokes occur, and hence the order in which the power strokes must also occur.

3 (*a*) The purpose of the clutch springs is to press the clutch plate firmly against the flywheel, and if they were weak they would not be able to do this, causing the clutch plate to *slip* on the flywheel when the pedal is raised.

(*b*) Driving with the foot over the clutch pedal should be avoided. In itself it does no harm, but the driver might put pressure on it *without being aware that he is doing so*. If this is done continually the clutch springs will weaken and 'clutch slip' could result. The fault is known as 'riding the clutch', but could not give rise to clutch drag.

(*c*) Insufficient play in the pedal can cause clutch slip because when the pedal is fully raised the clutch plate does not fully engage with the flywheel.

(*d*) Too much play in the pedal will cause clutch drag because when the pedal is pressed down the clutch plate does not come completely away from the flywheel.

4 (*a*) If the oil is too thin it will show a lower pressure as it will offer less resistance to the gears in the oil pump.

(*b*) Too much oil in the sump cannot affect pressure since, regardless of the *amount* of oil, the pump will only draw in enough at a time; it would, however, cause excessive oil consumption, as oil might enter the combustion chambers (forcing its way past the piston rings) and become burned.

(*c*) The most likely cause of excessively high oil pressure is that the pressure relief valve has stuck, so that it fails to allow oil to by-pass the pump gears when too much pressure builds up.

(*d*) Worn bearings would *reduce* oil pressure, as oil would escape through the bearings.

5 Wear in the cylinders eventually makes them oversized. They tend to become oval in shape because the pistons are constantly thrusting against one side of them. The result of this is that the piston rings no longer provide an air-tight fit, causing loss of compression, which in turn brings loss of power, since the latter is dependent on the former. Also, because the rings can no longer cope adequately with one of their jobs—preventing oil from passing the pistons—oil will be burned along with the mixture of petrol and air.

(*c*) Burning oil gives blue smoke, and so the combination of both this *and* loss of power would be the result. One remedy could be to fit oversized pistons to make good the discrepancy between pistons and cylinders.

(*a*) & (*d*) Black smoke, with or without loss of power, is indicative of burning too much petrol—in other words, the mixture is too rich.

(*b*) White smoke, with or without loss of power, means that the mixture is too weak, and is common on a cold winter's morning before the engine has properly warmed up.

6 (*a*) The operative word here is 'always'. An arrow engraved on a rotor arm does not *necessarily* indicate the direction of rotation. If a car has been acquired from someone else it is not impossible that at some time the previous owner replaced the rotor arm, and the replacement could bear an arrow having no relationship to the direction of rotation of this particular distributor spindle.

(*b*) If the rotor arm rotates clockwise the distributor should also be rotated clockwise to retard the ignition. The effect of doing so is that the segments inside the distributor cap, which convey the current from the rotor to the plug leads, will be moved *away from* the rotor arm. In other words, contact (or proximity) of the rotor arm and segments will take place later, and hence the ignition will be retarded.

(*c*) LT current is converted into HT current by inductance inside the coil box. This HT current flows through the lead to the centre of the distributor cap and from there passes through the carbon brush to the rotor arm. The rotor arm passes it to the sparking plugs. But, of course, it is *HT* current that is passed, and not LT.

(*d*) A hair-line crack in a distributor cap can most assuredly cause misfiring or even a complete failure. Dirt collects inside the crack and, being an effective conductor of electricity, shorts out a segment (or segments); instead of the current going to the segment (and thence to the plugs) it takes an alternative path through the crack. A hair-line crack may be indiscernible with the naked eye in daylight, but can be traced in the following manner:

Remove the distributor cap, but leave *all* the HT leads connected to it.

Remove the rotor arm and set the CB points closed.

Hold the cap upside-down in one hand and place the forefinger of your other hand into the centre recess on the under-side of the rotor arm (it should fit quite snugly).

Insert the rotor arm into the distributor cap (see diagram below) with the edge of the rotor arm immediately adjacent to *any* segment.

Have someone switch on the ignition and flick open the points. At this moment you will see the HT current flow from the rotor arm to the segment.

Repeat this procedure for each segment in turn.

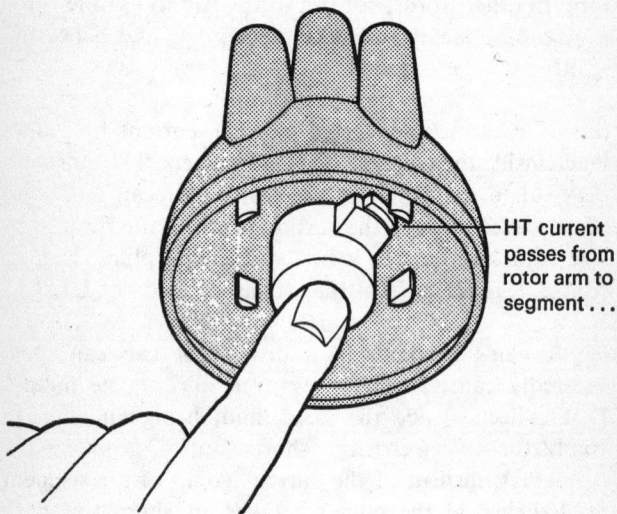

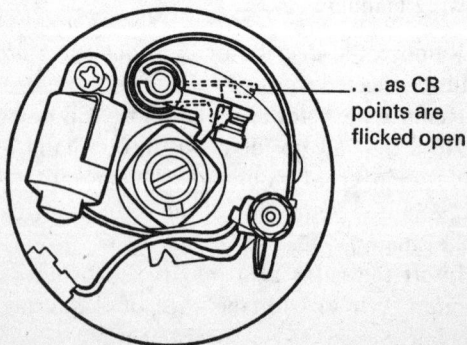

HT current passes from rotor arm to segment ...

... as CB points are flicked open

Should there be a hair-line crack in the distributor cap you will see the current passing through it like a miniature display of forked lightning.

If there is a hair-line crack in the distributor cap a 'get-you-home' remedy is to spray the interior of the cap with an ignition sealer. Aerosols containing ignition sealer are readily available, and every driver should carry one.

7 This is an unusual fault for headlights. More usual ones are: lights go dim when decelerating (battery partially discharged); failure of one light (faulty bulb or bad connection); lights fade (battery partially discharged); lights won't go on at all (battery disconnected or discharged). The most likely cause of flickering would be a loose connection or connections somewhere in the circuit, resulting in the circuit being made and broken from time to time.

(*b*) It is extremely unlikely (but not impossible) for a fuse to become loose in its holders, and this would be equivalent to a loose connection: the circuit would be periodically broken as the fuse broke contact with the holders. It could occur if, for example, a fuse broke and, lacking a spare fuse, a driver improvised by using a thin piece of wire or a piece of silver foil wrapped round the broken fuse (see question 5 in Test 1). If the improvisation were not carefully secured, vibrations of the car would cause the headlights to flicker as connection is made and broken.

(*a*) As stated above, if the battery is not fully charged the lights would dim or fade, but not alternately come on and go off.

(*c*) A loose fan belt could cause dimmed, but not flickering lights.

(*d*) It is hardly conceivable that both bulbs would become faulty simultaneously, and even if they did, they would fail altogether. Either the filaments would be broken or they would be intact, and light would either result or not, accordingly.

8 (*a*) Changing the position of the steering wheel on the steering column would not affect the turning lock of the steering, though it could put the spoke of the steering wheel in the wrong position and upset the indicator return mechanism.

(*b*) As explained in question 3, Test 6, the front wheels are connected together by the track rod, the ends of which (track rod ends) are adjustable for correcting the toe-in of the front wheels. This alters slightly the parallelism of the wheels, *but cannot* affect the amount of turning lock which they have.

(*c*) The drop arm is connected to the steering-box shaft and is in turn connected to the steering arm; according to the angle that the drop arm assumes, so the movement of the steering arm (and hence the turning of the front wheel) is influenced. Changing the position of the drop arm on the shaft can increase or decrease the amount of 'steering lock' available.

(*d*) Excessive play in the wheel bearings can cause the car to wander on the road and also wheel wobble. This dangerous fault should be remedied either by tightening the bearings or fitting new ones. But the wheel bearings influence the *rotation* of the wheels, and not the amount that they can be turned.

9 (*a*) There can be nothing wrong with the petrol pump if petrol is reaching the carburettor—and if it is leaving the inlet pipe to the carburettor it *must* be reaching it.

(*b*) A punctured float would give the opposite effect: instead of petrol *not* getting into the float chamber, *too much* would get in. The float would not rise on the level of the petrol and therefore would be unable to close the needle valve, which is responsible for cutting off further entry of petrol. The result would be that the carburettor would flood as the petrol overflowed the float chamber.

(*c*) As it has been established that no petrol is getting into the float chamber, the jets cannot come into the story. By the time petrol reached the jets it would have entered the float chamber, for how else could it get to the jets? A blocked jet would cause a weak mixture or even an engine stoppage simply because it would not permit petrol to pass through it.

(*d*) The needle valve alone regulates the flow of petrol into the float chamber (see question 7 in Test 5). As the float falls the needle valve opens and permits petrol to enter; when the float reaches a predetermined height it closes the needle valve and cuts off the petrol supply until more is needed.

Dirt in the needle valve might not only prevent the valve from opening but also block the entry of petrol.

10 Current flows from the unearthed terminal of the battery through the ammeter (if fitted) and the ignition switch. From the other side of the switch it passes to the SW (switch) terminal on the coil. Therefore, if the ignition key is lost, it is necessary to by-pass the ammeter and switch, and this can be done by connecting the unearthed battery terminal direct to the SW terminal. Naturally, it will be necessary to disconnect the wire in order to stop the engine.

If the wire were joined to the CB terminal on the coil, this would cut out the coil completely.

It would be no use connecting the wire to the earthed terminal of the battery; this would simply run the current straight to earth, and not through the circuit.

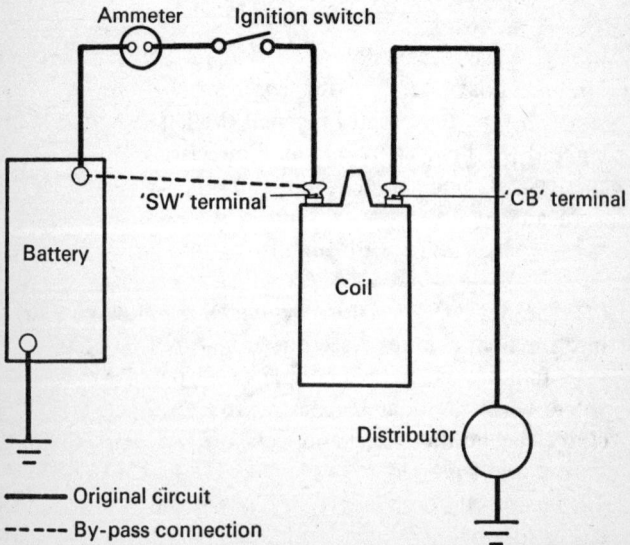

Ammeter — Ignition switch
'SW' terminal — 'CB' terminal
Battery
Coil
Distributor

——— Original circuit
----- By-pass connection

(On some coils the two LT terminals are marked + and −. The SW terminal is + if the battery is negative earthed, and − if the battery is positive earthed.)

Answers

Each correct answer scores 1 point.

Test 1 (*maximum score possible: 15 points*)

1 (*b*). **2** (*a*). **3** (*d*). **4** (*a*) FALSE; (*b*) TRUE; (*c*) FALSE; (*d*) FALSE.
5 (*d*). **6** (*a*). **7** (*c*). **8** (*b*). **9** (i) (*a*), (*b*), (*d*); (ii) (*b*), (*c*); (iii) (*b*), (*c*).
10 (*a*).

Test 2 (*maximum score possible: 13 points*)

1 Hotspot. **2** (*b*). **3** (*a*). **4** (*c*). **5** (*b*). **6** (*c*). **7** (*b*). **8** (*a*). **9** (i) (*d*);
(*ii*) (*e*); (iii) (*b*); (iv) (*f*). **10** (*d*).

Test 3 (*maximum score possible: 10 points*)

1 (*a*). **2** (*d*). **3** (*a*). **4** (*d*). **5** (*d*). **6** (*c*). **7** A—No. 3 lead, B—No. 4
lead, C—No. 2 lead. **8** (*c*). **9** (*b*). **10** (*b*).

Test 4 (*maximum score possible: 13 points*)

1 (*d*). **2** (*d*). **3** (*b*). **4** (i) (*a*), (*d*); (ii) (*c*); (iii) (*b*); (iv) (*e*). **5** (*d*).
6 (*c*). **7** (*c*). **8** (*a*). **9** (*a*). **10** (*a*).

Test 5 (*maximum score possible: 13 points*)

1 (*b*). **2** (*b*). **3** (*b*). **4** D. **5** (*a*). **6** (*a*). **7** (i) (*e*); (ii) (*a*); (iii) (*d*);
(iv) (*b*). **8** Ackerman. **9** (*c*). **10** (*c*).

Test 6 (*maximum score possible: 13 points*)

1 (*c*). **2** (*a*). **3** (i) (*b*), (*d*), (*h*), (*j*); (ii) (*e*), (*i*); (iii) (*a*), (*g*); (iv) (*c*), (*f*); **4** (*a*). **5** (*d*). **6** (*c*). **7** (*c*). **8** (*b*). **9** (*a*). **10** (*c*).

Test 7 (*maximum score possible: 13 points*)

1 (*b*). **2** (*a*). **3** (*d*). **4** (*c*). **5** (*c*). **6** (*a*) FALSE; (*b*) TRUE; (*c*) FALSE; (*d*) TRUE. **7** (*b*). **8** (*c*). **9** (*d*). **10** (*d*).

Pre-testing Analyses

The total number of points possible is 90, made up as follows:

Test	Points
1	15
2	13
3	10
4	13
5	13
6	13
7	13

Fifty drivers were time-tested. Learner drivers were not tested, as it was felt that the questions were out of their area, though it is possible that driving tests in the future will include a written test—probably on the lines of the tests in this book—and that some elementary knowledge of maintenance and mechanism will be expected.

The lowest number of points scored was 31; the highest was 72. The analysis of the individual tests was as follows:

Test	Lowest score	Highest score
1	4	12
2	3	10
3	4	9
4	5	10
5	4	9
6	2	9
7	3	11

The questions that received the fewest correct answers were:

Test	Question
1	8 and 9(ii)
2	1, 3 and 9(i)
3	6 and 7
4	4(iii)
5	2 and 7(iii)
6	3(iv) and 7
7	1, 8 and 10

The questions that received the most correct answers were:

Test	Question
1	10
2	8
3	1 and 8
4	3 and 8
5	1, 4 and 5
6	8 and 9
7	6(c), 6(d) and 7

The time taken for the individual tests was as follows:

Test	Shortest time (in minutes)	Longest time (in minutes)
1	5	9
2	6	10
3	4	9
4	5	9
5	7	11
6	8	13
7	5	12

From all the above it has been possible to evaluate:

Average score 45 points
Average time 54 minutes

How to Rate Your Knowledge

Add 5 to the total number of points you have scored and double the result.

If your original score is 45 points or more, ADD ONE POINT FOR EACH MINUTE UNDER 54.

Example 1

> Score: 61 points
> Time: 49 minutes

$61+5=66$, doubled$=132$, $+5$ time points$=$rating of 137.

Example 2

> Score: 53 points
> Time: 52 minutes

$53+5=58$, doubled$=116$, $+2$ time points$=$rating of 118.

If your original score is less than 45 points, DEDUCT ONE POINT FOR EACH MINUTE OVER 54.

Example 1

> Score: 43 points
> Time: 50 minutes

$43+5=48$, doubled$=96=$rating of 96.

Example 2

> Score: 43 points
> Time: 57 minutes

$43+5=48$, doubled$=96$, -3 time points$=$rating of 93.

In selecting the drivers for pre-testing, experts were not counted, since the idea was to test the 'average' driver. For this reason, car mechanics and police drivers were not included in the analyses, though it is interesting to note the following results from a car mechanic and a police driver:

Car mechanic

Score: 70 points
Time: 45 minutes
(Rating=159)

Police driver

Score: 82 points
Time: 47 minutes
(Rating=181)

Driving instructors were also excluded from the analyses, though one or two that were tested returned scores which were about average. The reason for this is obvious: although a driving instructor has to be expert in his field of teaching driving, he does not have to be an expert on car mechanism or maintenance. Usually he would know enough to maintain his vehicle and to diagnose common faults, but more advanced mechanical knowledge might well be out of his area.

The highest rating recorded was 135.
The lowest rating recorded was 81.

Index

Q = Question